FROM DISASTER TO DIVERSITY:
WHAT'S NEXT FOR NEW YORK CITY'S ECONOMY?

Edited by Jonathan P. Hicks and Dan Morris

Drum Major Institute for Public Policy

New York, New York

Printing by G&H Soho, Inc. in Hoboken, New Jersey.

Publication credits. An earlier version of Nevin Cohen's "Building An Urban Food System For The 21st Century" appeared in *City Limits* magazine. An earlier version of Justin Davidson's "Time For A New WPA? New York Needs Infrastructure—And Jobs" appeared in *New York* magazine.

Edited by Jonathan P. Hicks and Dan Morris. The editors want to acknowledge Andrea Batista Schlesinger for hatching the idea for this book in the winter of 2008 and enabling them to work together on such a fulfilling project. They also thank Mark Winston Griffith for his commitment and guidance during spring 2009; Lauren Su for her operations expertise and insight throughout all phases of the project; and Karin Dryhurst for her eagle-eyed copy-editing and proofreading as the book neared completion in fall 2009.

Questions, permissions requests, book orders, and media inquiries should go to:

Dan Morris
Drum Major Institute for Public Policy
40 Exchange Place, Suite 2001
New York, New York 10005
646.274.5713; dmorris@drummajorinstitute.org
www.drummajorinstitute.org

First Edition
Paperback print edition ISBN 978-0-615-33452-3

Book design by Hazan & Company

Photos: *Images are used under a Creative Commons license.*

Page iii: Egidio Bacigalupi/sxc.hu
Page 1:   Chris Suderman /flickr.com
Page 37:   Daniel Silva/sxc.hu
Page 67:   mike_w40/flickr.com
Page 89:   Tim Schnurpfeil/sxc.hu
Page 113:   Fabio Mascarenhas/flickr.com

CONTENTS

STRENGTHENING VULNERABLE COMMUNITIES

INTRODUCTION

By Jonathan P. Hicks

In the aftermath of New York City's 2009 campaign season, crammed with competitive primaries, a combative runoff and a prickly, startlingly close general election, New York City is now finally prepared to put aside the acrimony of the political process and place its focus on a central, pressing question: How will the city rebound from a crippling economic crisis?

This book can help guide what happens next.

The city's unemployment rate is higher than it has been since the early 1990s. Foreclosure is a realistic prospect facing tens of thousands of homeowners throughout the five boroughs. New York City is becoming increasingly polarized in a way that gradually but steadily separates residents according to their incomes. The city's budget deficit is flirting with the $5 billion mark. And more and more people feel pushed out of the middle class—as well as out of their neighborhoods.

Against that backdrop, there is undeniably considerable importance attached to how the controversial and historic third term of Mayor Michael R. Bloomberg will deal with New York City's gradual emergence from the most excruciating economic downturn in the better part of a century. This book offers a blueprint for governance by presenting a diverse and vivid set of plans on how the most critical components of the city's economy can be advanced and improved.

There are chapters here that look at the anchor industries of New York City—the financial sector and real estate market, for example. Some of the pieces contained here look at old industries through an utterly new-fashioned lens. They offer a fresh look, for example, at how the arts community could be bolstered and how media companies might retool for the second decade of this new century. And it proposes exciting ideas on how the city's still-vibrant immigrant communities might be better equipped to reach their economic potential.

The book casts a bright light on how development of a single tunnel might offer a jolt to the economy of the New York City region; how restructuring New York City's personal income tax might yield astonishing dividends and how, even in this age of Obama, race cannot be ignored in how public policy is crafted. It also looks at how a novel and unorthodox economic plan—the federal stimulus—can better attain its goals.

What is striking about the book is not just the scholarly power of the arguments and ideas that are being advanced here. It is also striking because of the diversity of voices. It includes offerings by elected officials, advocates, civic leaders and academics who, to say the least, might not be found in the same room, let alone in the same volume.

It is a wide-ranging collection that, if read without all the usual political caveats and calibrations, should enable elected officials, advocates and average residents to see what is really at stake when we talk about economic interdependence and shared progress—to overcome false divisions, embrace common ground, and pursue transformative action.

Whether they are traditionally partners in dialogue or challengers in dispute, they are unified by one central goal: to enhance the quality of life for the people of New York City, in every sector and neighborhood and across every conceivable demographic label.

Jonathan P. Hicks is a senior fellow at the DuBois Bunche Center for Public Policy at the Medgar Evers College campus of the City University of New York. He is a former political and financial writer for The New York Times.

ANCHOR INDUSTRIES, NEW BUSINESSES

NEW YORK'S FUTURE AS THE WORLD FINANCIAL CAPITAL

By Kathryn Wylde

N ew York City lost its seat as America's center of political power in what could be described as the first federal bailout, in the Compromise of 1790. This was a deal struck by Alexander Hamilton, Thomas Jefferson and James Madison, and accepted by President George Washington, in which the federal government agreed to assume the states' wartime debts. In return, the capital of the United States would move from Federal Hall, on Wall Street in Lower Manhattan, to an undeveloped site on the Potomac River on land that belonged to Maryland and Virginia. In the intervening years, there has been a healthy tension between New York City, America's acknowledged financial capital, and Washington D.C., the nation's seat of political power.

Today, as a result of the collapse of global financial markets and the federal government's role in the rescue of the banking system, the balance of political and economic power in America has tipped precariously in the direction of the Potomac. The government has become a major shareholder in many of the country's financial institutions and is proceeding not only to increase regulatory oversight but also to dictate the terms under which these businesses do business and compensate their employees. While most government leaders protest that nationalization of the banking system is not their objective, the extent of government control and intervention certainly approach that status.

The American public, meanwhile, wants to see blood run down Wall Street. They want the wings of the country's banking and investment sectors permanently clipped. This is bad news for New York

City, which needs to quickly reinvent itself as the new, more cautious, but equally creative world financial capital.

For much of the country, the financial services industry is simply a source of credit and capital to keep economies running. For New York City, finance is the core industry. It powered the city's resurgence from the urban crises of the 1960's and 1970's. Until this year, the FIRE sector (finance, insurance, and real estate) was responsible for about a quarter of the $1 trillion economic output of the New York metropolitan region. One in seven privately employed New Yorkers worked in financial services and the industry generated more than 17 percent of the city's income tax revenues.

The impact of the current financial system crisis on New York City has been staggering. The projected deficits in the city and state budgets for next year exceed $20 billion. In less than a year, a dozen of New York City's biggest financial firms disappeared, were acquired or converted to a regulated bank holding company. Through acquisitions and bank failures, control of much that remains of the industry has shifted out of New York and even out of the country. New York City is projected to lose about 80,000 jobs in the financial services industry by the end of 2010, with three-quarters of those jobs unlikely to return. Wage earnings in this sector are projected to decline by 30 percent in 2009 and a further 7 percent in 2010.

Trouble in the financial industry has spilled over into other sectors of the New York economy. The most robust sources of job growth during the past decade—professional services, retail, tourism, technology and entertainment—have lost customers and clients with the decline in financial service activity. The media sector, which depends heavily on revenues from advertising by automobile companies and banks, has been similarly devastated. Values of commercial and residential real estate markets have dropped more than 20 percent and contributions to philanthropy and the arts have decreased by 35 to 40 percent.

Many are appropriately calling for diversification of New York's economy, which is essential to withstand the boom–and-bust cycles of Wall Street. But there is no combination of sectors that can, in the foreseeable future, replace financial services as a source of high-paying jobs, economic multipliers and tax revenues. Although the industry likely will not be as profitable or contribute as generously to the regional economy and tax base as it has over the past decade, it remains essential.

Every great world city in the 21st Century global economy is a financial center, first and foremost. This is not appreciated in Washington, where the general consensus is that the car industry represents "real jobs" while the financial industry is merely razzle dazzle. New York needs to join with other American financial centers including Chicago, Boston, Atlanta, Charlotte and San Francisco—as well as our neighboring states of New Jersey and Connecticut—to make the case that financial industry jobs and products are both real and necessary to power the economy of the United States.

Maintaining New York's status as a financial capital begins with stabilization of the national banking system. This is well underway, as evidenced by the repayment of federal rescue funds, with interest and warrants, by 10 of the country's largest banks. Effective federal intervention and actions taken by leaders of the nation's financial industry have prevented what could have been a catastrophic collapse. President Obama has issued a proposal for comprehensive regulatory reform that will be debated in Congress and, if adopted, will help to restore investor and consumer confidence. This, in turn, will lead to more bank lending and consumer spending, accelerating national and local economic recovery.

Prompt action on regulatory reform will allow this country to define the framework for international actions to regulate global markets. Conversations are already underway with the G-20 nations that represent 85 percent of the world economy. New York stands to benefit from American leadership in an international regulatory approach that balances oversight with tolerance for risk and innovation.

On the other hand, federal actions that promote national protectionism are damaging to New York, which is first among the states in the number of jobs created locally by foreign companies. Some 15 percent of the city's economic growth in the past five years has come from foreign-owned businesses. "Buy American" provisions in the federal stimulus and threatened federal tax actions against foreign companies doing business in the United States effectively work against New York's position as a financial power and discourage foreign companies from listing on New York's exchanges. Last year, two Chinese banks chose New York as their American headquarters. And the expectation is that a major component of future growth will come from the expansion of New York as the western headquarters city for financial institutions from Asia and economically emerging countries. New York's economic future depends on federal policies that encourage foreign investment.

A prerequisite for New York's continued global leadership in financial services involves hanging on to the world's foremost aggregation of financial talent. PricewaterhouseCoopers and the Partnership for New York City publish an annual comparative analysis of world cities and their attractiveness to business, called Cities of Opportunity. The 2008 report determined that New York City was still ranked first in terms of intellectual capital, which is the single most important influence on location decisions in the 21st Century. New York also ranked first in technology and innovation and in lifestyle assets, both of which were important to talent retention. How much have the institutional casualties and job losses of the past year hurt the city's brand?

The March 2009 edition of London's Global Financial Centers Index, indicates that New York's brand remains strong. London's survey of financial industry professionals found that those who work in New York are more confident about this city's future as a financial powerhouse than they are about any other city. The index still ranks London and New York at the top of 62 financial global centers, even though both have lost some ground in the past year. Moreover, it concludes that the global crisis has had a notably worse impact on major centers in Asia than on the two western capitals.

Richard Florida, Professor of Business and Creativity at the University of Toronto, writing in the March 2009 issue of *The Atlantic*, argues that New York is more than likely to re-emerge from the current crisis as a financial leader because it is too far out front of the pack for other cities to overtake. The historic strength of the city's financial sector and the sheer concentration of talent in finance and related disciplines, such as law and technology, give New York the best chance for continued dominance. Professor Florida also concludes that New York's openness to talent and the diversity of its economy will help the city to exit this crisis re-energized.

Retention of top talent cannot be taken for granted, however. Federal restrictions on executive compensation and limitations on the ability of financial companies to secure H1-B visas are substantial barriers to recruiting the best global talent. Already, the governments of China and the United Arab Emirates are reaching out to hire New Yorkers who are victims of financial layoffs. Recognizing the threat, New York City and state government are taking proactive steps to establish services for connecting unemployed professionals to jobs, educational programs and entrepreneurial opportunities. Ultimately, however, winning the fierce international competition for talent will require aggressive public-private partnerships that engage industry and all levels of government.

In what will be a tougher competitive environment, New York City's status as a financial capital also depends on decisive action being taken to contain taxes, litigation liability and energy costs. New York has some of the highest business taxes in the country. The need to raise revenues to close city and state budget gaps may push the city beyond the tipping point when it comes to tax tolerance. To enhance its status as a financial center, New York needs to expand tax revenues through economic growth, rather than increased tax rates and new assessments. New York is also among the states where business feels most vulnerable to law suits and punitive regulation. This has a particular chilling affect on attracting new companies that are not already heavily invested here.

Finally, high energy costs discourage power intensive technology companies from setting up shop here. Future job growth depends on addressing all three issues.

Assuming the basics are addressed, there are plenty of ways New York can leverage its financial industry for economic development, methods that it has ignored in the past. For example, a number of multinational corporations are re-examining the benefits of "back-shoring"—that is, bringing back office technology centers and support services home from overseas locations. The cost differentials that made it attractive to take jobs offshore are diminishing. With strategic incentives and thoughtful marketing, the highly productive talent pool in New York, especially upstate, could be very attractive for financial industry support operations.

Ironically, regulatory reform will also lead to new business activity and job growth in New York City's financial sector. Senator Charles E. Schumer has called for a restructured Securities and Exchange Commission to operate out of New York, where it can draw on talent that understands both the industry and the products being regulated. President Obama's proposal that the new systemic risk regulator should be run under the Federal Reserve Bank also promises increased regulatory activity in New York.

Administering the complex federal programs intended to jumpstart the national economy requires the expertise of the private sector, a fact the Treasury Department acknowledged in its procurement procedure. Already, major New York firms are involved. Bank of New York Mellon was named custodian of the Troubled Asset Recovery Program funds. Goldman Sachs and Blackrock have won roles as investment managers for the program to purchase agency mortgage backed securities and JP Morgan Chase is the custodian.

New York's most entrepreneurial young companies are also taking the initiative to develop innovative products tailored to the new regulatory environment. Creditex, a startup launched in 1996 with funding from the New York City Investment Fund and a consortium of New York-based financial institutions, has won federal approval to operate a clearinghouse for trading of credit default swaps. Recently acquired by Intercontinental Exchange, Creditex has more than 500 employees in New York and it anticipates future growth as part of the effort to bring transparency to derivatives markets.

Federal stimulus and stabilization programs present increased affirmative business opportunities for the large number of minority- and women-owned financial companies headquartered in New York. Helping these companies get federal contracts and subcontracts is one way to redeploy talent from Wall Street and build a new layer of successful financial enterprise in the city. And thanks to the downsizing at the largest investment banks, smaller firms can now afford to recruit talent previously beyond their reach.

Opportunities for public-private partnerships are another area where New York investment firms and not-for-profit institutions can make a particular contribution. New York pioneered the nation's affordable housing and community development movement, establishing the prototypes for the programs that restored the vitality of America's urban neighborhoods. This has been recognized by the Obama Administration in tapping New Yorkers for key housing and urban policy positions. The Rockefeller Foundation has recently begun funding an effort to insure that New York's experience is applied to restructuring over-mortgaged multifamily apartment buildings that are part of the toxic asset inventory of lenders and investors. These efforts could be the basis for renewing and expanding the city's community development and lending industries.

New York City and New York State are taking action to enlist the wealth of New York-based educational and research institutions to help advance sector-specific economic development strategies—something other states have done far better in the past. Up to now, it has been the Massachusetts Institute of Technology that held a preferred relationship with the financial industry when it came to applied research and developing the next generation of financial technology. Stanford enjoyed similar status on the West Coast. Governor David A. Paterson has announced a new program to provide incentives for university and business partnerships like the financial technology applied research and education center established by both JP Morgan Chase and Syracuse University. Mayor Michael R. Bloomberg has announced a business incubator project with New York University-Polytechnic which will provide a locus for financial and software engineering innovation by local entrepreneurs.

New York-based IBM, NYSE Euronext, Nasdaq OMX Group, Bloomberg LP, Thomson Reuters and McGraw Hill are examples of thriving innovators at the cutting edge of financial information and technology. Matched with New York's engineering, technological and entrepreneurial talent, these companies can expand the footprint of Wall Street to encompass a new range of financial information and technology jobs.

Venture capitalists report that there is a cluster of entrepreneurial activity focused on financial technology in three American cities: New York, Chicago and San Francisco. Some are targeted at using technology to make big companies more efficient in the current cost-conscious environment—processes known as virtualization and optimization. Others are crossing the lines between media, telecommunications and finance. All represent growth sectors in the global economy where New York has the assets to excel.

In sum, the underlying strength of the city's institutions, its diversity, its depth of talent, and its internationally respected brand all suggest that New York will survive and continue to thrive as a world financial center. Going forward, New York's financial services industry will almost certainly be more inclusive, more entrepreneurial and more diverse than before the financial crisis of 2008. The Gordon Gecko stereotype from the film *Wall Street* is one that the American public loves to hate. But such characters will not survive the new regulatory and business environment. Nonetheless, New York will remain America's gateway to the global economy and the place that political leaders in Washington will need to draw upon for the financial acumen and business resources required to sustain America's position as an economic power.

Kathryn Wylde is president and chief executive officer of the Partnership for New York City.

AS OLD MEDIA STRUGGLES, OPPORTUNITIES IN NEW MEDIA EMERGE
By Jon Whiten

You no longer have to be a media insider relentlessly checking Jim Romenesko's media news blog to understand that the news media industry is struggling. Over the past few years, we've seen bankruptcies, newspapers and magazines closed, and countless layoffs. On her excellent Paper Cuts blog, Erica Smith estimates the number of layoffs and buyouts at American newspapers between July 2007 and today at 31,425.

And while the industry's nosedive has coincided with the global economic downturn, the media's problems are far greater than one recession might produce. The industry has to struggle with the evolving media landscape and the continual encroachment of digital technology, much of which cuts into profits traditionally reserved for the mainstream—and alternative—media.

The federal Bureau of Labor Statistics' job growth estimates bear this point out. In the bureau's most recent occupational outlook handbook, the job category "news analysts, reporters, and correspondents" is expected to grow just 2 percent between 2006 and 2016. That's at the same time that the number of job seekers will undoubtedly continue to increase. But in the "financial managers" sector, which has certainly taken a hit in the last few years as Wall Street jobs have evaporated, there are expectations of growth by about 13 percent over the same period.

Here in New York, where the overall media industry employs more than 300,000 workers (nearly 10 percent of the city's private workforce), the *New York Sun* ceased publication in September 2008;

The New York Times has cut hundreds of jobs and reduced salaries; countless magazines have folded and there is an air of gloom hanging over much of the industry.

But all is not lost. Many forward-thinking writers, editors, tech geeks and publishers are quickly adapting to changing circumstances, with some actual success.

Take the SoHo-based *Huffington Post*, for example. The website, which was launched in May 2005 with a staff of "half a dozen," has grown to employ more than 50 people. HuffPo's success, it could be argued, has stemmed from its decision in 2006 to move the focus from aggregating the opinions of public figures to employing actual journalists to do original reporting. (Former *Newsweek* editor Melinda Henneberger was the first such hire in November 2006.)

Since then, the site's traffic has grown from about 2.3 million visitors per month to more than 7 million unique visitors per month. With the increased traffic, the site has been able to raise additional venture capital, and—most importantly for this discussion—hire more journalists. The site currently maintains a roster of dozens of editors and reporters, including longtime old-guard journalists like former *Washington Post* staffers Tom Edsall and Dan Froomkin.

The success of HuffPo does have a dark underside, however. While the site should be applauded for expanding its original reporting and experimenting with pro-amateur collaborative efforts like Off the Bus, which paired unpaid contributors with professional, paid journalists, it is still built on the backs of the approximately 4,000 bloggers who contribute—for free—to the site.

This poses several problems. First, as Michelle Haimoff pointed out in July 2009, it creates an "increasingly homogenous" voice for the site and has the potential of alienating those who don't identify with that voice. More importantly, as Haimoff—herself an unpaid HuffPo blogger—noted, "the only writers that will write for free are writers that can afford to write for free."

So what's the fix? Haimoff suggests a performance-based bonus system for the site's unpaid contributors—a model that has been employed at other web publishing ventures like Gawker Media's sites.

But such a system is flawed and adds unneeded additional pressure to an already high-pressure profession and ultimately erodes the idea of job security.

"We're working in the digital equivalent of a sweatshop," one disgruntled Gawker Media blogger wrote in 2008 (before being fired soon after).

Slate editor Jacob Weisberg, talking to Online Journalism Review in 2005, noted that this type of system could easily lead to pandering and sensationalism, and would also be bad for worker morale. "It would create an unproductive kind of competition among our writers," he said.

Some, like CBS Sports, have suggested employing a similar metric, but tied to "visitor loyalty" rather than raw page views. But this still gets back to a performance-based pay system that could ultimately be exploitative.

The real solution here is bigger than any individual website's pay structure; it ultimately lies in the macro level: how news media organizations make money. While some leading thinkers and big-name publishers like Rupert Murdoch have suggested an online pay wall is necessary to preserve both media institutions and the jobs they provide, a plan recently launched by New York Mayor Michael R. Bloomberg takes an even wider approach.

Bloomberg's office estimates that his initiatives—part of the larger MediaNYC 2020 program—will create roughly 8,000 jobs and help grow the city's media industry. The plan rightly has a strong eye toward the future and technological innovation, with a heavy focus on technology and bringing new media investment to the city, which has long been a global center for old media institutions.

Among the initiatives are the creation of a NYC Media Lab, a research center that will work to connect media companies and academics, modeled after the successful labs at MIT and Stanford University. The administration is also launching a program to help local companies learn the ins and outs of bidding on city government contracts, a high-tech center for media freelancers in lower Manhattan, a digital media training program for "displaced or entrepreneurial" media workers, a competition for web developers who use city data to create useful applications, a bond program for information technology purchases and a fellowship program for entrepreneurs.

One of the most exciting initiatives of the research center is the media and tech fellowship, which will go to 20 "rising star" entrepreneurs each year. These fellows will receive mentoring, access to venture capital firms, and support services like legal aid.

The Bloomberg plan is right to focus on small media businesses, especially when it comes to web publishing and other technological applications that can be less labor-reliant than traditional media production. But you don't have to be high-tech to be small and successful in the news media industry.

Recent surveys from trade groups like the Inland Press Association and the Association of Alternative Newsweeklies (disclosure: that's my employer) show smaller papers suffering far less than their larger counterparts. Some small papers are actually reporting positive revenues, an anomaly worth cheering.

In New York, there are many small newspapers, ranging from community weeklies like the *Norwood News* or the *Brooklyn Paper* to the nearly 400 newspapers represented by the New York Community Media Alliance (NYCMA), which focuses on the "immigrant and community press."

NYCMA executive director Juana Ponce de Leon told NPR in April 2009 that her organization's newspapers were doing pretty well, all things considered.

"Their revenues are down, however, it is not the same type of dilemma that is facing the mainstream corporate media," she said. "This media sector in the main has been accustomed to functioning with very little resources."

And that scrappy ethos is one thing that these small newspapers have in common with web-based startups. The other key similarity: They often have tight audience focus. They might not have the widest distribution, but they have engaged readers and, more importantly, they often have a sort of monopoly on information about a particular subject or ethnic group.

As web publishing proliferates, serving a particular niche or particular immigrant community is one of the clearest ways for a publication to survive and thrive.

"Yesterday's approaches to news are failing to educate, enlighten, or inform... It's time for a better kind of news," Umair Haque recently wrote on the Harvard Business Review's website.

He says the answer lies in the economic model of niche publications, a model now known as nichepapers.

"Nichepapers offer more bang for the buck: greater benefits for far less cost," Haque writes. "Readers get more, better, and faster content— while publishers realize lower capital intensity, lower distribution, marketing, and production costs, and less risk."

Mr. Haque's point is well-taken, but it's worth looking at from another angle. Can these nichepapers sustain—and even create— middle-class media jobs? Or are we about to enter an age of journalism where everyone is an entrepreneur but we all struggle to make ends meet?

While I just don't see nichepapers and new media outfits creating the kind of robust, middle-class careers in media that the mainstream organizations have in the past, there is a strain of hope.

As smaller institutions gain more traction and take readers away from the "old media," the old media needs to put up a fight. These outlets need to learn from the new competition rather than dismiss it outright. The growth of not only bloggers but technology experts in a research and development division at *The New York Times* is an example of the step in the right direction.

While not all of these positions are what might have traditionally been considered "journalism" jobs, they are jobs, and well-paying ones at that. Coupled with the proper educational initiatives and robust training programs for young people, there's hope that when the digital transformation is all said and done, plenty of worthwhile career paths in news media will remain.

Jon Whiten *is editor of the Association of Alternative Newsweeklies.*

IMMIGRANT ENTREPRENEURISM: AN ENGINE FOR ECONOMIC RECOVERY
By Jonathan Bowles

With New York City's financial sector expected to lose 65,000 jobs in the current economic downturn, it's more apparent than ever that the city needs to diversify its economy and nurture new sources of job growth. While it's difficult to predict which industries will give the city the economic jolt it needs, it's a good bet that immigrant entrepreneurs will provide a key spark to the city's recovery.

Immigrants have a long and storied history of starting businesses in New York. But their contributions have grown in the past decade or two, thanks to a nearly unprecedented wave of new immigration to the city. During that period, immigrant entrepreneurs have gone from being a mere footnote in the city's economy to a powerful engine of economic growth. Foreign-born entrepreneurs have been starting a greater share of new businesses than native-born residents, stimulating growth in sectors from food manufacturing to health care. In doing so, they have created loads of new jobs and have transformed once-sleepy neighborhoods into thriving commercial centers.

Nationwide, immigrants are nearly 30 percent more likely to start a business than non-immigrants, according to a November 2008 study by the United States Small Business Administration. Another recent study showed that more than half of start-up technology firms in Silicon Valley were founded by immigrants over the last decade. My own research for the Center for an Urban Future reveals that immigrants drove all of the growth in New York City's self-employed population between 1990 and 2000: the number of foreign-born individuals who were self-employed increased by 64,001 (a 53 percent jump) while the number of native-born people who were self-employed decreased by 15,657 (a 7 percent decline).

The Center's 2007 study also found that neighborhoods across the city in which many, if not most, businesses are immigrant-owned witnessed an explosion of new enterprises over the past decade that far surpassed the rate of business creation citywide. Between 1994 and 2004, the number of businesses citywide increased by less than 10 percent, while the number of businesses grew by 55 percent in Flushing, Queens; 47 percent in Sunset Park, Brooklyn; 34 percent in Sheepshead Bay-Brighton Beach, Brooklyn; 25 percent in Elmhurst, Queens; 18 percent in Manhattan's Washington Heights neighborhood, and 14 percent in Jackson Heights, Queens.

Job growth in immigrant-dominated communities also far outpaced overall employment gains. Between 1994 and 2004, overall employment in the city grew by just 7 percent, but rose by 34 percent in Washington Heights, 28 percent in Jackson Heights, 23 percent in Sunset Park, 13 percent in Sheepshead Bay-Brighton Beach, 12 percent in Flushing and 10 percent in Elmhurst.

While immigrant-run companies have already become extraordinary catalysts for economic growth in the five boroughs, they could become even more integral to New York City's economy in the future—and pivotal to resuscitating the city's faltering economy. After all, foreign-born individuals now make up 37 percent of the city's population and are expected to continue to drive much of the city's future population growth. This alone suggests that they will be an increasingly important economic force. At the same time, local economic development officials have barely begun to unlock the full potential of the city's immigrant entrepreneurs. The contributions made by immigrant-run firms, while immense, have occurred with virtually no support from city policymakers and despite the fact that immigrants often face enormous obstacles to starting and growing businesses here. With just a little support, this could be a much more potent source of future growth.

There is reason to believe that New York is not reaching its potential with immigrant-owned businesses. Only a relatively small number of immigrants who own restaurants or other retail businesses have expanded into larger space or opened stores in additional locations. Most vendors never give up their pushcart in favor of becoming a store owner; few businesses that make unique ethnic products have attempted to export to other states where recent immigration patterns have created a market for those goods; and large numbers of immigrant-run firms in New York remain narrowly focused on serving their own ethnic community rather than pursuing greater ambitions in larger markets.

There is also evidence that fewer immigrant- and minority-owned businesses in New York City grow to the next level, as compared to their counterparts in other cities. Of the 15 American cities that have the most Hispanic-owned businesses, New York has the lowest average receipts per establishment. The average Hispanic-owned company in the five boroughs earned just 37 percent as much as a Hispanic-owned business in Houston, 40 percent of the average in Chicago and 42 percent of the average in Miami. Similarly, New York City's Asian-owned businesses took in a smaller amount of receipts, on average, than their counterparts in 13 of the 15 cities with the most Asian-owned businesses. The average Asian-owned company in New York City earned 48 percent as much as a similar establishment in Los Angeles, 57 percent of one in Houston and 71 percent of one in San Francisco.

While immigrant-run businesses in New York City may be less likely to grow than their counterparts in other cities, many foreign-born entrepreneurs in the five boroughs struggle simply to survive. Some go bankrupt after a short existence and others toil in an endless struggle to stay afloat. Many are tripped up by the same factors that hamstring other small businesses in New York, from the high cost of commercial real estate and insurance to the city's overzealous regulatory enforcement agents. Others find it difficult to succeed simply due to intense competition or because their business model isn't sustainable.

But immigrants also encounter a long list of problems unknown to most native-born entrepreneurs—such as unfamiliarity with how business is done in this country, lack of awareness about local regulations, limited financial literacy and, often, little or no credit history. Language barriers add another element of difficulty for numerous immigrant entrepreneurs. Unable to communicate effectively, immigrant entrepreneurs are less likely to attempt to sell goods and services in markets beyond their own ethnic communities, or to seek assistance from established small business assistance providers. Without such help, many immigrant business owners take bad advice from friends, family or accountants, and make costly mistakes. Others turn to professionals who speak their language but who take advantage of them.

Harnessing the potential of immigrant entrepreneurs will require greater attention and support from city economic development officials and the many nonprofit community organizations, chambers of commerce and business assistance groups that work with small businesses around the five boroughs. These entities should be well positioned to help immigrant entrepreneurs overcome these challenges and develop systems that enable them to grow. Unfortunately, too few of the city's established economic development entities have effectively connected with immigrant populations. Meanwhile, immigrant entrepreneurs remain mostly detached from the city's overall economic development strategy.

Fortunately, there's some cause for optimism. Mayor Michael R. Bloomberg recently unveiled a new set of initiatives designed to support small businesses and promote entrepreneurship. Among them was a plan to create a loan fund that might help microfinance organizations increase the number of loans they make to immigrant entrepreneurs.

Yet, much more could be done. The city's Department of Small Business Services and the New York City Economic Development Corporation should develop a new framework for providing business services to immigrant communities. Right now, too few of the programs overseen by the business services agency are reaching immigrant entrepreneurs.

Both entities should also partner more with local organizations that have credibility in immigrant communities. Any plan to provide business services to immigrant entrepreneurs must start with the understanding that countless numbers of legal immigrants will never seek assistance from a government-run center—and that many won't set foot into a nonprofit organization they don't trust.

As part of this, city and state officials should expand their support for microenterprise organizations. These entities—from ACCION New York and Seedco to the Business Outreach Center Network—already have the expertise to support immigrant entrepreneurs but often lack the capacity to serve additional clients.

Finally, city economic development officials should take new steps to ensure that more of the city's immigrant entrepreneurs expand into larger businesses. One option is to help local immigrant-run businesses export their products beyond the five boroughs. A major opportunity lies with the scores of businesses throughout the five boroughs that manufacture unique ethnic products, import foreign goods for distribution, or provide specialized services to immigrant communities. Many of these companies could easily expand their operations—and create new jobs—by exporting their goods and services to other parts of the country that have emerging immigrant populations but few ethnic businesses of their own. With minimal support, some of the city's small immigrant-run firms might become the next Goya Foods or Golden Krust.

Jonathan Bowles is director of the Center for an Urban Future, a nonpartisan think tank based in New York City. He is the co-author of the Center's 2007 study about immigrant entrepreneurs, entitled "A World of Opportunity." That report is available at www.nycfuture.org.

TRANSFORMING THE CITY'S MANUFACTURING LANDSCAPE
By Adam Friedman

I magine that it's a hot, steamy Sunday morning. You're in bed looking out the window at a hazy, grey sky. You hear the low, constant rumble of trucks crossing the Hudson, laden with everything the city needs to survive.

You get up and drag yourself into your kitchen. You put a frozen bagel in your toaster and a spoonful of instant coffee in your cup. You want to go out to buy a newspaper. But instead you sit in front of your computer to read the Sunday news because nothing is printed any longer in New York.

You have a ticket to the last art gallery in New York, something you've waited months to see. You look in your closet through the newest Wal-Mart mix-and-match separates but nothing inspires.

You're finally ready to venture out but you're limping. There is no excitement, no anticipation of the unexpected, the newness, the edginess that city life once brought.

This is not my beautiful New York!

The smog, fatigue, environmental and cultural degradation just envisioned comes not from an over abundance of manufacturing and industrial uses, but from their absence. Imagine if everything the city needed to survive had to be trucked in—if every inch of our waterfront had been developed into luxury condos and we lost the capacity to barge in materials and the ability to make the comforts and quirky pleasures of urban life here in the city.

There are 7,000 manufacturing companies in New York City. You may not see them or the almost 100,000 people who work for them. But they are here, not only maintaining the basic necessities that every city needs, but adding to the diversity, creativity, allure and energy that is New York's greatest competitive advantage, and helping to maintain New York's sustainability.

If the city is serious about its commitments to reducing its carbon footprint, to increasing the use of recycled materials and to retrofitting its building stock to reduce energy consumption, then the city needs local manufacturers to create green products and transform its waste into usable resources. Furthermore, if New York is to grow its creative engine, it needs to maintain the diversity of spaces, jobs and people that inspires creativity. If the city is to cut the income disparity that has come to characterize New York's economy and offer more paths into the middle class, it needs to create well-paying manufacturing jobs and offer affordable space for industrial entrepreneurs.

THE INVISIBLE MIDDLE CLASS SECTOR

In the New York City of the 1950s, it was hard *not* to know someone who worked in a factory. There were more than 1 million manufacturing jobs in New York, roughly one of every three workers.[1] While there were factories in every borough, the greatest concentration was in Manhattan where office workers and factory workers crammed the subways together. The one- and two-family neighborhoods of Queens, the Bronx and Brooklyn were built by, and largely for, workers who were making their way from the shop floor to production supervisor to manager.

Manufacturing is far less visible today in New York City. The drop in manufacturing employment and growth of other sectors has reduced the profile and relative importance of manufacturing. The geography of manufacturing has changed, with both market forces and numerous zoning changes pushing manufacturing out of view. Today, manufacturing jobs are primarily held by people of color, who make up 69 percent of the city's manufacturing workers, and immigrants, who account for 66 percent.[2] If there is any doubt of the veracity of those statistics, one need only observe the Greenpoint Avenue or 36th Street subway stations in Brooklyn at 7 a.m. on a weekday; streams of Latino and African-American workers come through these stations, heading to their manufacturing jobs nearby. The relocation of jobs to the outer boroughs, the shift in demographics, and the drop in employment, have combined to reduce the sector's visibility.

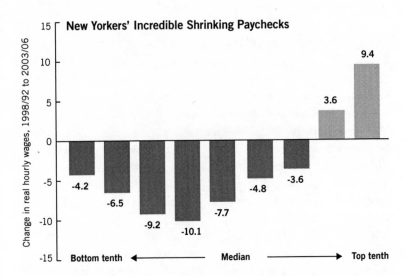

New Yorkers' Incredible Shrinking Paychecks

Source: One City, One Future (2008) National Employment Law Project, New York Jobs With Justice and The Pratt Center for Community Development. Analysis of data by the Fiscal Policy Institute

The experience of physical work, of making a tangible product, and of being in industrial neighborhoods is now fairly limited among New York City's population. Yet there are 100,000 manufacturing jobs, 120,000 jobs in other industrial sectors such as transportation, warehousing and utilities. And there are another 200,000 jobs in construction and wholesaling—a full sixth of the city's private employment.

These hundreds of thousands of industrial jobs are pathways to the middle class for many families, particularly for people who lack educational credentials. Manufacturing jobs pay $52,000 on average— 49 percent to 121 percent more than the average retail and restaurant jobs.[3] Yet 34 percent of the manufacturing workforce does not have a high school degree.[4] Study after study rightly points to the drop in manufacturing employment as one of the root causes of New York's growing income disparity and the shrinkage of the middle class. In addition, manufacturing provided an economic ladder that helped immigrants and low-income families climb into the middle class. And these studies have fueled the argument that the city must do more to preserve—and even grow—this sector.[5]

MANUFACTURING AND THE ECONOMY IN NEW YORK

As 2008 drew to a close, New York and many other urban areas around the country and the world experienced the volatility of an economy driven mainly by the financial sector. By early estimates, New York has already suffered more than other cities because of our dependence on financial services. It is extraordinarily ironic that the city is now suffering because it has ignored the cardinal rule of financial management: Diversify. Don't put your savings in any one investment. Urban economies are no different.

Across the country, there is growing public support for rebuilding our manufacturing base. It is a core component of the emerging federal economic policy that investment in energy efficiency and renewable energy should be used to not only improve the country's basic competitiveness, but stimulate business and job growth in the industries that make the hundreds of component parts for renewable energy systems.

The green energy sector is only one area with the potential to generate production jobs. Cities throughout the United States whose economies were built on manufacturing are developing strategies for their industrial sectors. For example, Chicago and Los Angeles have emphasized the retention and attraction of manufacturing as a key economic strategy for economic diversification. But local production is not only a means to economic diversity; it holds environmental, cultural and social benefits to a city.

HIGH-VALUE MANUFACTURING IN NEW YORK

In January 2003, Mayor Michael R. Bloomberg spoke about the high cost of doing business in New York City. "If New York City is a business, it isn't Wal-Mart... It's a high-end product, maybe even a luxury product. New York offers tremendous value, but only for those companies able to capitalize on it."

Some interpreted the mayor's remarks to mean that New York was only for the rich and therefore city policy could disregard the middle class and their business and employment needs. But there is another interpretation that reflects what is already happening on the ground in our city and offers a chance to build upon our unique local advantages.

The truth is New York City will always provide a high-cost business environment. However, businesses in all sectors can adapt to New York's high costs by producing high value-added goods and services to provide middle-class and decent entry-level jobs. This strategy is as true for manufacturing as it is for the arts, legal and financial services and other sectors of the economy. In manufacturing, value-added represents the difference between the cost of raw materials and the value of the final good due to how the materials have been transformed (for example, pieces of wood and metal worth a couple of hundred dollars are worth tens of thousands when they are made into a Steinway Piano). The good part is that high value-added businesses generally lead to higher wages because the workers are the ones adding a good share of that value to the end product.

New York's manufacturers are the best in their industries. They have to be in order to survive. It is not cost-effective to manufacture low-value goods like staplers in a high-cost environment like New York City. In the diamond industry, New York jewelers cut only the largest stones and send the small diamonds to be cut abroad—who has time for a small diamond? New York apparel manufacturers work with the city's designers to produce samples or couture that retails for $5,000 and more. The *schmatte* business is gone but the fashion business still thrives.

High-value means several things. First, workers' skills in transforming raw materials into finished goods—typically learned on the job over many years—lead to high wages. Second, proximity makes direct face-to-face communications between customers, their design resources and the manufacturer possible. Proximity makes "quick turn" production possible—a good business model in a town that does not have time to add the word "around" to the phrase. Proximity is also freshness—nobody wants a croissant that has been sitting on a truck for more than one hour, two at the most. Third, high-value is design, care, craft or culture, which can include technology but is not necessarily high technology, as anyone who has purchased Der Dau boots, a Ferrara metal chair or a Scrapile wood table knows. [6]

The density, diversity and wealth of New York's marketplace create a natural incubator for high value-added businesses. But this does not mean local manufacturers serve only the New York market. The base may be here but they also export to niche markets throughout the country which in themselves may not be large enough to support an industry. For example, New York food manufacturers (which tend to be specialty producers nurtured by local immigrant markets) export $1.6 billion worth of locally manufactured foods (about 34 percent of total sales).[7]

The transformation of the New York City manufacturing sector into a smaller but very high-value added set of businesses may offer lessons for the city's handling of the financial services sector. The loss of larger manufacturing operations that made relatively low-design, commodity products like staplers (Swingline), electrical switches (Eagle) and pots and pans (Farberware) was largely inevitable. They no longer had a business reason for being in New York. Proximity to the market and design talent did not justify the cost of a New York location.

THE ENVIRONMENTAL NEED FOR MANUFACTURING

The notion that a healthy manufacturing sector is necessary to promote New York's environmental well-being may at first seem counterintuitive. Buried in our conception of manufacturing are images of dark factories belching smoke and pouring hazardous waste into our waterways while workers are abused below the heels of greedy bosses.

While the toxic remains of manufacturing's past continue to contaminate brownfields around the city, today's manufacturers are fundamentally different. The smokestacks that manufacturers previously needed to generate their own power are gone, replaced by modern utilities or their own renewable energy supply.[8] Government regulation has largely forced manufacturers to clean up. Low-road companies moved abroad to low-wage areas, which also tend to have minimal environmental protections.

Now, a new business model and culture based on sustainable business principles is emerging. This business model is often described as having a "triple bottom line" that measures not only profit but the environmental and social impact of the business. A sustainable manufacturer seeks to reduce waste not only because it reduces the costs of materials and disposal, but because it also consumes less of our planet's resources and will help the manufacturers expand their markets to consumers concerned about the environment.

In the Brooklyn Navy Yard (an industrial park owned by the city), IceStone takes recycled glass and makes it into granite-like slab material that can be used as kitchen and bathroom countertops. Five years ago, IceStone employed five people and today it employs 50. "We're going to double in three years" says Peter Strugatz, IceStone's Co-CEO. "The crazy part of this business has been that we have had to buy our glass from the Midwest and truck it in. Local glass is collected, co-mingled, broken and mixed with rotting organics, which mixes the colors and makes it almost worthless for commercial uses." To create a source of local glass for both the company and for other manufacturers, IceStone recently created IceGlass, which is attempting to establish a glass processing facility that will create glass of higher value that is color-sorted, cleaned and crushed. This glass would be made available for high-value products that can be reused.

Elsewhere in the Yard, a biodiesel company is setting up a factory to collect waste cooking oil and grease from restaurants in the City. The waste will be reprocessed so it can fuel diesel engines. Another company is building a solar and wind powered streetlamp and designing extremely energy efficient light bulbs.

To attract these green manufacturers and to set an example for others, the Yard itself is greening its operations. New buildings are built to the Leadership in Energy and Environmental Design (LEED) standards promulgated by the U. S. Green Building Council to assess the sustainability of a building. The Yard is also installing solar and wind generators and looking for other ways to reduce waste and energy consumption to reduce its total carbon footprint. Finally, the Yard is developing approximately 1 million sq. ft. of new industrial space.

There are a variety of forces driving the growth of local green manufacturing and creating opportunities for a healthy green manufacturing sector. One of the most important factors is increasing and unstable energy costs. The other is the absolute imperative to reduce carbon emissions, which may soon be embedded in American law. These factors are combining to increase transportation costs relative to other cost factors. Historically, transportation costs have fallen continuously as people harnessed water and wind, then coal and rail, and then oil and diesel to move goods.[9] The consumption of increasingly scarce and expensive fossil fuels and the almost unfettered release of carbon into the air are coming to an end, and that will lead to changes in transportation patterns and costs.

Shifts in public policy can also spur growth in manufacturing. Governments at all levels are increasingly supporting business practices that hold manufacturers responsible not only for the production but also for the disposal of a product—a product's "life cycle."[10] For example, this past year the New York City Council passed legislation that will require manufacturers of electronic equipment such as computers, printers and cell phones to develop programs to retrieve and recycle their customers' electronic waste. The European Union is already developing pilot programs and standards for the recovery and recycling of such "e-waste." This may lead not only to product redesign to facilitate disassembly and reuse, but may impact how manufacturers choose a location for their businesses. In the past, manufacturers only had to factor in the cost of transporting a product to the consumer. Now, there may be the cost of a return trip. These forces are pushing the "point of production" to coincide with the "point of consumption."

THE CHALLENGES TO NEW YORK'S MANUFACTURING SECTOR

Study after study concludes that space is the primary challenge to retaining and growing the city's manufacturing sector.[11] The real estate challenge is really three interrelated problems: insufficient space for the number of industries that want to be in New York City; unstable real estate conditions fostered by antiquated zoning; and a mismatch between the needs of small companies and the space which was built for larger traditional manufacturers.

There are about 250 million square feet of industrial space in New York City, which seems like a lot. But the areas zoned for manufacturing in New York must also accommodate a variety of other extremely land-consuming uses essential to the basic operations of the city. This includes the city's airports, subway yards, utilities, oil and gas storage tanks, as well as the warehouses that keep our food and other essentials in close reach. While the vacancy rate for industrial space is not tracked as carefully as it is for residential and office space, there is abundant anecdotal evidence: There is no vacant space at the Brooklyn Navy Yard and the industrial parks each report vacancy rates under 5 percent. Over the past 5 years, the city has rezoned approximately 20 million square feet of space and an additional 12 million are in the pipeline to be rezoned from manufacturing to other uses. Approximately 20 percent of the city's industrial land will have been rezoned within a few years.[12]

Even in those areas zoned for manufacturing, the current Zoning Resolution permits other non-industrial uses that can price out manufacturing. Manufacturing is a high-value added activity because a manufacturer's major investments are in labor and equipment. They have little money left over to pay for land, which means manufacturers pay low rents relative to other uses, leaving them vulnerable to displacement.

Offices, hotels and most types of big box superstores are permitted as-of-right in manufacturing zones. As a result, there are now at least 52 hotels in industrial areas including twelve in the city's industrial parks, areas that the city has designated to be preserved for industrial uses. The city is pushing to encourage development of supermarkets in manufacturing areas which could become the anchors for new retail clusters. The city definitely needs more supermarkets, just not in its manufacturing areas.

The result is not only direct displacement, but real estate speculation by the property owners which undermines investment by the tenants: If a property owner thinks he can attract a developer offering to buy his land for an office, hotel or superstore, the owner will set his asking price accordingly. Real estate speculation makes manufacturers question the future of their locations as an industrial neighborhood and that uncertainty discourages reinvestment, thereby triggering a downward spiral.

Allowing the remaining manufacturing zones to be destabilized or converted could have disastrous consequences both for neighborhoods and citywide. Industrial areas tend to be walk-to-work communities where local residents are also local workers—particularly in Sunset Park, Chinatown, North Brooklyn and the South Bronx. Converting manufacturing space to retail replaces well-paying jobs with low-wage, often part-time jobs. In the long run this process takes wealth out of the adjacent residential communities undermining the residential quality of life as well. And the mode of development is hardly sustainable—big box stores increase traffic and consume large areas of land for surface parking, a situation in part required by a zoning resolution that has parking requirements developed when the Studebaker and Packard still roamed our roads.

On the most basic level, New York needs cement plants, barge ports, food warehouses and other essential logistical support services to keep functioning. Above that, it needs bakeries, coffee roasters, apparel manufacturers, woodworkers, and glassblowers to keep it inspiring.

WHAT NEW YORK CITY SHOULD DO

In 1961, New York City enacted its current Zoning Resolution. Gas cost 31 cents per gallon[13] and John Glenn had not yet orbited the earth. It would be four years before the New York World's Fair would open, nine years before the first Earth Day and 16 years before Ed Koch would be elected Mayor.

An awful lot has happened since then that was not foreseen, changing many of the fundamental assumptions underneath our zoning. In 1961, there were no superstores, front and back office operations were located together and oil companies gave away glasses, steak knives and cash prizes to lure people into buying more gas. Smoke and other harmful emissions poured out of factories. Building highways was seen by some as the way to bring New York City back from a decade of population decline.

The Zoning Resolution was based on defining and separating incompatible uses to keep the then-noxious manufacturers from pushing into residential and other commercial areas. The underlying economics and environmental standards were such that residents and other businesses needed protection from manufacturing but manufacturing did not need protection from other commercial uses which today can push them out. The Resolution took such an extreme stance toward use separation that it sought to minimize the pattern of mixed land uses that then existed—and in some cases, existed comfortably—in many communities.

The City's Zoning Resolution reflects a bygone era. New zoning tools should be added to create balanced mixed uses districts which would allow a variety of uses to coexist but not drive out any one use and tip a community toward homogeneity. This will benefit not only the sectors related to the "creative economy" but the growing freelance sector, many of whose members work at home.

Another principle is the need to preserve diversity of space because we are entering a period of dramatic transformation with unpredictable twists and turns. The next big growth sectors will probably reflect the need to adapt to a low-carbon economy. In the beginning of human society, energy came from people and animals. Then we harnessed the resources of our environment, particularly those that were carbon-based, starting with coal but rapidly changing to petroleum and natural gas. Now we need to develop clean energy sources, retrofit buildings and change some of the fundamentals of our society's operating systems. It's time for Society 3.0. But after that, who knows?

The city we envision should be bursting with creativity and entrepreneurial energy so that whatever the challenge and opportunity, New York City has both the intellectual capacity and the industrial infrastructure to capitalize on it. It must keep its edginess and diversity and continually improve its environmental standards to attract and stimulate generations of entrepreneurs.

GROWING A GREEN SECTOR

The most obvious opportunities for growth are driven by our transition to a low-carbon economy. The Bloomberg Administration has articulated an extraordinarily ambitious vision for a more environmentally-friendly city through PlaNYC. The investment anticipated by that effort in everything from the retrofit of buildings to renewable energy generation to mass transit could be leveraged to stimulate a cutting-edge green industrial sector that creates living wage jobs.

First, the city should strengthen the supply chains that will provide the materials and goods for the projects stimulated by that investment. For example, it should identify the products and materials that go into retrofitted buildings, from energy efficient windows, doors and lighting fixtures, to motion sensors and smart meters. Then it should look at the local industrial base to identify how much of that could be locally made and provide the technology, engineering assistance and space local manufacturers need to compete for this work.

Second, the city has incredible buying power—$16 billion of procured goods in fiscal year 2008—a force that could be harnessed to stimulate local companies to reinvest and reposition themselves to capitalize on this opportunity. The city should create a modest 5 percent or 10 percent discretionary price preference for locally manufactured goods purchased by the city. For example, if a company is bidding on a city contract, will provide a product manufactured in New York along with living-wage jobs and is within 5 percent of the lowest bidder who is providing a product made further away, the city could award the contract using local manufacturers. The preference might sunset after several years to create a temporary transition period to provide companies with a chance to retool and reposition as part of the larger strategy to strengthen supply chains.

Local should not be limited to New York companies, a geopolitical standard, but to products manufactured within a certain number of miles (such as 100 miles or 200 miles) from New York. The rationale for this approach is that it reduces the carbon footprint by reducing trucking, allows companies within a large market to compete but still stimulates local production and the use of local recycled materials.

Fourth, in the end, all businesses have to be green, which will require a tremendous cultural shift within the business community. Routine business behaviors that encourage extravagant packaging ignore the availability of recycled and recyclable materials, use hazardous or carbon-based products when safer alternatives are available have to give way and be replaced by adoption of sustainable business practices.

The city can support this transition by weaving "green strings" and sustainable business practices into its economic development programs.[14] Significant public support for companies should be matched by those companies adopting significant green upgrades. Businesses receiving low interest loans to acquire and construct buildings through the Industrial Development Agency (IDA) should be required to build to LEED standards. Renovations using IDA financing should include major energy conservation measures or renewable energy generation. Companies doing business or receiving more modest benefits from the City should be required to engage in more modest steps, for instance producing and regularly updating an "Environmental Policy Statement" that spells out each company's plan to improve its operations and environmental compliance.

PROVIDING SPACE FOR GREEN JOBS

It is pointless to invest in green jobs if they have no place to go.

In New York, Mayor Bloomberg took the first steps in 2005 by creating the Industrial Business Zones program which designated 16 areas of the city for industrial development. The strategy was to create "safe havens" in order to stabilize real estate conditions in these areas by declaring the City's intent to keep them industrial. Unfortunately, the initiative did not include revisions to the Zoning Resolution. In Williamsburg, Gowanus, and Long Island City factories have been redeveloped as hotels, bowling alleys, and large retail. In Flatlands, a 500,000 square foot distribution site on a rail line is being turned into a Home Depot.

The city needs to plug the holes in the Zoning Resolution which currently allows hotels, offices and big box retailers in Manufacturing Zones and to bring it up to date with new city policy. The City should reinforce the Industrial Business Zone designation through Industrial Employment Districts[15], a new zoning that would not allow non-industrial uses in its industrial safe havens. This would stabilize the real estate market in those areas which would lead to reinvestment and job growth. The Department of City Planning has edged in this direction in two small zoning changes in the South Bronx and in Dutch Kills in Queens where it limited hotel and retail uses and offered density bonuses for expansions of manufacturing uses. It is time to make this policy citywide.

Second, the city also needs to use zoning to reinforce its mixed residential/industrial neighborhoods such as Greenpoint and Williamsburg which are exactly the type of creative communities that attract and stimulate new ideas. For years, a special zoning district balanced industrial and residential development, preventing either use from completely displacing the other and preserving the diversity of spaces and uses that underlie creativity. However, the zoning was not effectively enforced during the 1990s and illegal residential conversions proliferated. The city subsequently changed the zoning to allow unrestrained residential conversion and development, leading to both the loss of diversity and displacement of both manufacturers and artists.

Third, the city should reverse its policy of selling off its industrial properties and should assume long-term management with the goal of creating high quality manufacturing space for job intensive sectors. In the past, the city has either sold off these sites to individual companies (both manufacturers and others) or leased them out with relatively low demands for industrial job creation or allowed them to lie fallow because the city lacked capital funding to renovate.

Fourth, the city should manage more of its industrial properties through mission-driven non-profit organizations such as the Brooklyn Navy Yard Development Corporation (BNYDC) and the Greenpoint Manufacturing and Design Center.[16] BNYDC currently manages the 300-acre city-owned industrial park at the site of a former U. S. Navy base. Other city-owned industrial sites could be managed by BNYDC and other independent non-profits like the Greenpoint Manufacturing and Design Center. The success of the BNYDC and GMDC non-profit model is in part their ability to focus on their mission, to allow senior staff to exercise discretion and take risks in developing strategies to advance that mission, and in being able to work directly with the individual tenant companies so that they understand their companies' needs and can help capitalize on opportunities.

Fourth, in addition to transferring management of its industrial properties to these organizations, the city should use them to help address the mismatch between the existing building stock, which was originally developed for large manufacturers, and today's need for smaller industrial spaces. This could be done both through the acquisition of sites such as the recently shuttered Pfizer plant in Brooklyn, or through joint ventures and partnerships with private owners who are willing to maintain industrial properties but lack the resources to renovate and manage the space.

Finally, as part of the Environmental Impact Statement (EIS) process the city should evaluate whether proposed land use change advances or sets back the City's overall sustainability. For example, each barge that brings material into the city replaces 50 trucks. Continued re-zoning of the waterfront for residential use could undermine the city's ability to implement more environmentally responsible trans-portation practices.

The question "what keeps New York City attractive?" for people brings us full circle to the need to retain manufacturing to ensure the city's diversity and creative vitality, its environmental well-being, and the employment and entrepreneurial opportunities that are pathways out of poverty.

Adam Friedman is Director of the Pratt Center for Community Development and was previously the executive director of the New York Industrial Retention Network. Mr. Friedman sits on the Boards of the Brooklyn Navy Yard Development Corporation and the Community Services Society.

Endnotes

1   Kagann, Stephen. "New York's Vanishing Supply Side" *City Journal*. Autumn 1992. http://www.city-journal.org/article01.php?aid=1514.

2   2006 American Community Survey PUMS via Infoshare.org. For production occupations, 79 percent of workers are people of color and 74 percent are immigrant. For production occupations in manufacturing, 82 percent are people of color and 79 percent are immigrant.

3   NYS Dept. of Labor QCEW dataset. Wages are annual average wages for 2007 and are based on total payroll costs, which includes costs of fringe benefits.

4   2006 American Community Survey PUMS via Infoshare.org. 38percent of workers in production occupations do not have a high school degree, and 44percent of workers in production occupations in manufacturing industries do not have a high school degree.

5   The most recent report is *Reviving the City of Aspiration*, Center For An Urban Future, February 2009.

6   This analysis is not to suggest that some standardized products could not be manufactured in New York under the right circumstances such as having relatively low space requirements and using materials coming out of New York's waste stream.

7   *Not Just A Link In the Food Chain*, NYIRN, p 14.

8   An extraordinarily ironic role reversal is that today it may be cleaner and cheaper for factories to install their own solar roofs and gas-fired cogeneration systems then to take electricity from the grid.

9   Edward Glaeser and Janet Kohlhase estimated that transportation costs dropped 95percent in real terms over the 20th Century because of the truck and highway systems. See "Cities Regions and the Decline of Transportation Costs," July 2003.

10   This strategy has already been successfully applied under federal environmental protection law to the use and disposal of hazardous waste.

11   *The Little Manufacturer That Could*, NYIRN, 1999; *Protecting and Growing New York City's Industrial Base*, New York City Economic Development Corporation (2005)

12   See *Protecting New York Threatened Manufacturing Space* (2008) The Pratt Center.

13   U.S. Department of Energy, http://www.eia.doe.gov/emeu/aer/txt/ptb0524.html.

14   The City already regulates the behavior of its purchasing agents and the companies with which it contracts such as by encouraging them to use minority- and women-owned businesses. Why not green businesses?

15   Industrial Employment Districts have been advocated by the Zoning For Jobs Coalition which includes more then 50 community groups, labor unions and economic development organizations.

16   The author, Adam Friedman, is a member of the Board of Directors of the Brooklyn Navy Yard Development Corporation.

DEVELOPMENT, GROWTH, AND STIMULUS

RECOVERY WITH A NEW VISION FOR ECONOMIC DEVELOPMENT
By Annette Bernhardt, Brad Lander and Carrie Brunk

As New York City grapples with a contracting economy, deepening strains on government resources, and turmoil on Wall Street, those who make economic policy are understandably focused on the most urgent necessities—bringing budgets into line, reviving growth, and providing aid to struggling families and the unemployed. But to focus only on immediate problems is to repeat the mistakes of the past, mistakes that have helped put New York City in its current economic predicament.

Even during the city's remarkable boom following 9/11, and now as we struggle with a serious recession, one fact has remained constant: the city's economic development policies simply haven't been working for many New Yorkers.

Over the past two decades, wages rose for the wealthiest fifth of the population but remained flat or dropped for everyone else, even as the costs of housing, energy, food, and other essentials grew sharply. At the same time, the city and state's main growth strategies—ambitious real estate development projects, billions of dollars in subsidies to industries that didn't need them—have exacerbated the strains on ordinary New Yorkers while creating new ones. Rezoning and city-led development projects have led to out-of-scale construction that most communities can't embrace. Job growth has been concentrated in industries such as restaurants and retail, which pay low wages and offer no benefits. Sectors that pay higher wages, such as manufacturing and transportation, have seen nothing close to the support that real estate developers have received.

And that was during the good times. Today, the formula for growth that City Hall and Albany have embraced is no longer reliable or productive. In a credit crisis, coupled with shrinking demand for offices and condominiums, the future of real estate megaprojects is in doubt. The finance sector is likely to emerge from the current meltdown much smaller in scale, meaning that New York City will have to turn elsewhere to generate jobs and revenue. And the failure of city and state government to nurture healthy housing markets in our neighborhoods is now undermining both the city's economic health and the quality of life.

So where do we turn now? Can we use this moment to define a new economic development framework, one that gets us out of recession and off the inequality path and instead delivers living-wage jobs, affordable housing, and sustainability, which are essential to the health and welfare of our city?

We would argue that New York City can—and indeed must—find a new paradigm for how it goes about driving growth during good times and bad. Just as it did with PlaNYC, its far-reaching agenda for strengthening the city's infrastructure and environment, the city needs to step back, revise its strategy, and lead the way with ambitious policies and long-term investments that build communities as well as the economy. We need to measure our city's success based not just on real estate prices and economic output but also on New Yorkers' ability to earn enough to raise a family and to provide neighborhoods with the infrastructure they need to thrive.

While public and private capital for development will continue to tighten in the short term, stimulus investments and other actions toward recovery promise a revival in economic activity—and the need to be prepared with policies to make sure that the benefits of growth will be enjoyed more widely in the future. In *The Audacity of Hope*, President Obama writes of a need for "prosperity that is shared," an idea whose time has come in New York City as well as the nation. Economic policies must take measures to ensure that the gains of government investment in infrastructure and the economy are enjoyed by all, not to be plucked by those actors best trained in financial engineering, government lobbying, and the art of finding financial gain in others' economic weaknesses.

New York City would not be the first American city to seek policies that aim to accomplish these goals rather than waiting in vain for prosperity to trickle down. In Los Angeles, for example, economic development projects that get public funding must create living-wage jobs, affordable housing, and more resilient neighborhoods. In Seattle, construction projects must provide apprenticeship opportunities for local residents. In Washington, D.C., workers in one of the city's fastest-growing occupations—security guards—now get paid a living wage, plus benefits. Also in Los Angeles, labor unions and government agencies are collaborating on green job training. San Francisco has a citywide minimum wage and requires affordable housing in new development projects. On the other side of the Atlantic, London is governed under a master plan that calls for development to promote economic opportunity.

Just as President Obama and Congress developed an economic stimulus package that centers on infrastructure investments, education, and green energy, New York City must also identify strategies that put people to work. In the federal stimulus plan, New York City will receive between $4 billion and $5 billion dollars—money explicitly meant to put New Yorkers to work on productive public and private projects. The city and state will have discretion about how to use much of that money. And both need to do it in a way that improves New Yorkers' quality of life as well as their economic prospects.

For example, retrofitting housing for energy efficiency will create jobs while achieving cost savings for homeowners and, with the right incentives in place, for tenants. Bringing supermarkets and healthy food to low-income communities builds on untapped market potential. The cross-harbor rail tunnel planned to connect freight train lines in New Jersey with Brooklyn and Queens will relieve neighborhoods of noxious truck traffic while increasing the flow of goods in and out of the city. Living wages for underpaid service workers will send more money coursing through their neighborhoods' economies.

Such policies have not restrained growth in the cities that have adopted them. On the contrary, they provide a foundation for further economic success. Over and over again, the lesson from policy innovations on the ground is that setting standards and investing for the long run pays off—and that conversely, short-sighted practices to cut costs can end up generating larger costs down the road. Our fuel bills are skyrocketing because tens of thousands of old buildings are not energy efficient. We spend nearly $600 million a year on emergency shelter for the homeless. Low-wage workers are forced to rely on public support systems like food stamps and Medicaid to make ends meet for their families. By contrast, when workers are paid better, they stay on the job longer, gain experience, become more productive, and save employers the cost of recruiting new workers. Retrofitting buildings can both benefit environmental sustainability and create thousands of new jobs. Ensuring that New York's families have enough affordable housing provides not only immediate stability but also strengthens the broader social fabric of our neighborhoods.

In short, increased standards and strategic investments aimed at improving our jobs, housing, and communities have the potential to yield substantial economic and social benefits. A more public, accountable process for how government invests its economic development resources will help ensure that those benefits are shared widely and targeted where the need is greatest.

It is this type of broad vision that over the past several years has animated the emergence of an accountable development movement in New York. While still scattered across various constituencies and issue areas, advocates have succeeded in elevating the central question—development to what end? —squarely into the public arena.

One of these efforts is the "One City/One Future" network, which over the past three years has involved dozens of civic groups, neighborhood advocates, community development organizations, labor unions, affordable housing groups, environmentalists, immigrant advocates and other stakeholders. Most recently, the network released *One City/One Future: A Blueprint for Growth that Works for All*

New Yorkers, outlining a full menu of concrete policy tools to redirect economic development policy in New York City.

Here, we want to highlight the three anchor goals that underpin this blueprint and that in our minds should serve as the central frame of reference for New York City as it paves a path to recovery over the next several years:

GOAL 1: RAISE THE STANDARDS

Government should set clear standards for economic activity in New York City, especially activity that benefits from public spending or actions. Meeting these standards—whether they concern the quality of jobs created or the environmental sustainability of new buildings—must be a prerequisite for anyone doing business with the city. The public should expect more from employers, developers and land owners—especially those doing business with city government or profiting from government action. By asking them to do their part, we can ensure that all New Yorkers share in the benefits of growth.

Specifically, here are three areas where stronger standards are both viable and sensible as part of an economic recovery strategy:

Public spending and actions: The city and state should ensure that when government resources are used to promote economic development, concrete public benefits result. New York should make the creation of middle-income jobs, quality affordable housing, and livable communities the central goals of its economic development agencies and programs.

Low-wage jobs: Many of New York City's fastest-growing industries—including restaurants, retail, building security, home health care, and child care —pay very low wages. New York needs to begin the process of upgrading these jobs by shifting these industries towards providing better wages and benefits.

Consumer services: The city and state need to ensure that New Yorkers who are buying homes, seeking jobs, or borrowing or investing money are working with qualified advisors who are acting in their interests.

GOAL 2: INVEST FOR SHARED GROWTH

The city and state currently spend billions of dollars to keep New York's economy humming. These investments in housing, transportation and employment need to be designed and managed with the explicit objective of improving opportunity and strengthening neighborhoods. Targeted public spending can help strengthen our economy and yield significant returns for New York's working families and their communities. Investing in workforce development, for example, can lead to higher employment rates, reduced spending on public assistance programs, and a stronger economy; investments in transportation and housing in areas of the greatest need can allow residents to spend more time and resources in their communities.

Specifically, here are four areas where targeted public investments are timely and can be integrated with federal recovery programs:

Job training: New York City's economic development system must connect city residents—especially those who face significant obstacles to employment—to jobs and career opportunities through a coordinated job readiness, training and apprenticeship system. Through investments in programs that expand access for lower-income communities, communities of color, immigrants, and the unemployed and under-employed, all segments of the workforce can share in the jobs and training opportunities generated by economic development.

Low-wage jobs: The city needs to develop targeted strategies for upgrading the low-wage jobs in which more than 1 million working New York adults today spend their careers. The city should invest in improving wages and job standards and create career ladders to better-paying positions for the workers who make our city run.

Neighborhoods and community assets: New York City needs to make expanding affordable housing, transportation, and economic security part of its economic development strategy.

Energy efficiency and green economic development: New York City's monumental commitment, through PlaNYC, to greening the city offers a rare opportunity to build a city that's not just environmentally sustainable but also economically prosperous. The city should foster equitable green economic development by growing emerging green industries that offer well-paying jobs with accessible career ladders for the city's workforce.

GOAL 3: REFORM THE PROCESS

Planning and development must take place in an open and democratic environment, in which communities and the city work as partners, not adversaries, with the objective of building a prosperous city on the strength of livable neighborhoods. Land use and economic development decision-making must be a collaboration between government and the people of New York City, involving meaningful public participation, full transparency of the finances and activities of publicly funded entities, and stronger support for community boards and other civic organizations that enable the public to participate. The city's own economic development agenda must be guided by thoughtful assessment of how benefits and burdens are distributed across the neighborhoods, classes, and racial and ethnic groups of New York City.

Specifically, there are three areas where accountability and transparency reforms are most important:

The economic development process: In spending billions of dollars of public money on subsidizing economic development, New York City must commit to transparent and publicly accountable processes and to ensuring that the benefits of those investments are shared broadly.

Land use policy: The city needs to dramatically alter its policies surrounding land use planning. City planning decisions must be made collaboratively with communities, on the basis of a shared and comprehensive framework that treats all neighborhoods fairly and provides the necessary infrastructure to sustain growth and strengthen communities.

Manufacturing and small business: Rapid increases in real estate costs and zoning that favors residential development have undermined companies that provide good blue and green-collar jobs; small businesses; and startup companies looking to expand in the city. The city needs a comprehensive set of policies aimed at preserving affordable space for manufacturing jobs, small businesses, and the new green industries that we need for a dynamic 21st Century economy.

Shifting economic development in New York City to these three goals—raising standards, investing for shared growth, and reforming the process—will not only take time; it will require a strategic prioritization of policies that complement and buttress the goal of economic recovery. Here are two current examples of development-related initiatives that are in their early phases but that would be highly effective:

BRINGING GOOD FOOD AND GOOD JOBS TO UNDERSERVED NEIGHBORHOODS

Low-income neighborhoods in cities across the country suffer from a chronic shortage of quality supermarkets—and a chronic shortage of good jobs. In New York City, the problem is especially acute as rising commercial rents have led more and more supermarkets to close in low- and middle-income neighborhoods, leaving residents with bodegas, drug stores, and other low-quality food options (and the poverty wage jobs that often accompany these options).

The Department of City Planning recently documented that 3 million New York City residents live in "food deserts," defined as neighborhoods that lack quality full-service supermarkets. Residents of these neighborhoods have limited access to a full range of quality food such as fresh produce, meat, and dairy. And they often pay higher prices than other New Yorkers for the groceries that are available. Studies have shown that the scarcity of supermarkets in these neighborhoods has serious health consequences for New York City residents, including increasing rates of obesity and diabetes. And these health consequences have a serious fiscal impact, as New York State spends $6.1 billion annually to treat obesity-related health problems.

The food desert problem has been widely documented and recognized by cities and states across the country. However, to date, most solutions do not address the lack of well-paying jobs for families living in these neighborhoods, despite the fact that quality supermarkets can create jobs that pay good wages and provide health benefits.

In New York City, a coalition of community organizations and labor unions recognized that bringing quality supermarkets to low-income communities was an opportunity for New York City neighborhoods to improve the health of its residents by solving the food desert crisis *and* by creating higher paying jobs with benefits. Thus, these advocates—including the United Food and Commercial Workers Local 1500, the National Employment Law Project, the Pratt Center for Community Development, and Good Jobs New York—began developing a city policy to address the chronic shortage of quality grocery stores and quality jobs in the city's low-income neighborhoods.

The policy focuses on using the city's economic development tools to encourage "high-road" supermarkets—supermarkets that provide quality food, pay good wages, and provide affordable health benefits to their employees—to open new stores in underserved communities. While studies have repeatedly demonstrated that supermarkets can and do profit in low-income neighborhoods (because high population density offers concentrated spending power that is comparable to or even higher than that of suburban areas) barriers exist—such as high rents, difficulties obtaining financing, and struggles to find adequate space—that make it difficult for high-road supermarkets to take advantage of these untapped markets.

To help high-road supermarkets locate in underserved communities, the proposed policy would, among other things:

• Provide a "one-stop shopping" resource for potential supermarkets to receive technical assistance on city and state incentives and city land use regulations, and provide a user-friendly guide of all city, state, and federal subsidies available to supermarkets;

- Allocate pre-development grants of up to $50,000 to help potential supermarkets defray the costs of environment site assessments, surveys, appraisals, and options;

- Award performance-based subsidies to supermarkets who meet food and job quality standards to be returned to the city if these standards are not met;

- Require supermarkets utilizing these programs to report and make public employment data information, including data on the jobs, wages, benefits, and residency of their employees;

- Include a supermarket requirement in larger city requests for proposals (RFPs) for development of city-owned land, so that developers in areas that have appropriate zoning and square footage requirements for a supermarket are obligated to include a high-road supermarket

As these advocates recognize, bringing high-road supermarkets to underserved communities is a unique opportunity to address the shortage of quality food and quality jobs in New York City's low-income neighborhoods. And in addition to the immediate impact of better health and higher wages, these new supermarkets, once built, have the potential to spur even more economic development. A standard 30,000-square-foot supermarket often provides between 100 and 200 new jobs, and by attracting complementary stores and services, supermarkets often serve as anchors for other businesses.

REDEVELOPING CONEY ISLAND WITH GOOD JOBS, AFFORDABLE HOUSING, AND A VIBRANT PUBLIC SPACE

The future terms for the redevelopment of one of New York City's greatest treasures, Coney Island, have been set. But as the Bloomberg administration pushed through the area's rezoning earlier in 2009, community, labor, and cultural groups with a stake in the future of the area came together around a groundbreaking collaboration that built on the ideas and alliances developed through One City/One Future. No matter what the outcome of the Coney Island rezoning, this recognition that good jobs, affordable housing, livable communities, environmental sustainability, and cultural vitality can and should coexist will remain an influential force in shaping future New York City development practices.

Seeking to bolster the lively but faded historic amusement area by the beach in Coney Island, the Bloomberg administration initiated a zoning plan intended to encourage the development of bold new entertainments as well as development that could generate revenue from the world-famous strip at the southern edge of Brooklyn. Over the protests of many planners and preservationists as well as community residents, the zoning proposal sets aside a significant amount of land for luxury condo towers and hotels. The city's plans also envision development on the site of the city-owned KeySpan Park parking lot but do not call for any meaningful public benefits such as affordable housing or living wage jobs or public space or even space for amusements, in exchange for that valuable real estate opportunity.

As the city's development plan emerged, the Pratt Center for Community Development and Jobs with Justice—two of the three partners coordinating One City/One Future—began to convene neighborhood, housing, labor and cultural groups with a stake in Coney Island's future to identify core principles for Coney Island's future development. How could they use the land use process to commit the City to provide needed benefits for the neighborhood?

Following a careful assessment of neighborhood needs, the groups ultimately agreed that they would support a development plan that:

- Guarantees good jobs with responsible contractors and employers for local residents in every stage of the project;

- Ensures that at least 40 percent of the housing created or preserved is affordable to low-, moderate-, and middle-income New Yorkers—with at least half of the affordable units reserved

for families at or below the median income for households in
Coney Island;

- Preserves and strengthens the "people's playground" through
an open, affordable, and vibrant amusement area with spaces
for vendors and small businesses, and investments in historic
resources; Creates much-needed public amenities for local
residents of the area, including a school and a supermarket
to meet local demand and significantly improved public
transportation.

Based on realistic and pragmatic anticipation of opportunities to be
brought by Coney Island's future development—and mindful of the
need to encourage its development not hinder it—the groups pro-
ceeded to recommend specific measures to reach those goals:

- Rigorous labor standards, including the use of responsible
contractors, prevailing wages, training and apprenticeships,
first source hiring for local residents, and labor peace
agreements, as well as measures to promote disclosure and
enforcement of compliance;

- Firm commitments to the inclusion of housing affordable to
a diverse range of incomes on both City- and privately owned
land, such as designating 80 percent of new housing on City-
owned land for affordable units and half of affordable units for
local residents;

- A larger free and open amusement area that incorporates
more historic preservation and commitments to opportunities
for small vendors and retailers, with fees collected for use of
individual rides and amusements;

- Community amenities that include at least one new school,
a large full-service supermarket, and public transportation
improvements.

★ ★ ★

In this time of turmoil, we see an important and compelling window of opportunity to change how we manage our economy—and with Wall Street on the ropes, such change is now also a necessity. Even during the recent economic boom, most New Yorkers did not get ahead financially. In the current economic crisis, they are falling even further behind.

But both our own history and innovations in other cities prove that we have significant power at the local level to respond and build a stronger city, that we can commit ourselves to an economic development model that brings better jobs, more affordable housing, and deeper environmental sustainability. The end result will be a transparent, accountable development process in which communities partner with the city to bring development and growth in ways that are welcomed and needed.

There is no doubt New York City and state can do this—but we need strong leadership and commitment from all the stakeholders involved. Through much of its history, New York City has been a national leader in promoting policies designed to improve quality of life, strengthen urban neighborhoods, and promote economic opportunity and a more cohesive city. To do that now, we have to advance our most vital resource—the New Yorkers who build, serve, aid, counsel, process, assemble, sell, and create, and make the city run. New York City now has not only the opportunity but the obligation to apply its resources and innovation to build a foundation of shared prosperity for coming generations.

Annette Bernhardt is Policy Co-Director of the National Employment Law Project. Brad Lander is a Senior Fellow at the Pratt Center for Community Development and a newly elected City Councilman in Brooklyn's 39th District. Carrie Brunk is Executive Director of New York Jobs with Justice.

One City/One Future is a collaboration led by the National Employment Law Project, New York Jobs with Justice, and the Pratt Center for Community Development, and endorsed by 65 civic groups, neighborhood advocates, community development organizations, labor unions, affordable housing groups, environmentalists, immigrant advocates, and other stakeholders in New York City's economy. The One City/One Future Blueprint for Economic Development is available for download at www.onecityonefuture.org.

THE NEED TO FUEL ECONOMIC GROWTH WITH DEMOCRATIC PLANNING

By Peter Marcuse

E conomic growth requires planning. But planning is about more than economic growth. New York City, for at least the last several decades, has nevertheless equated the two. And it has done so with a very narrow definition of economic growth, in which the crucial question—growth for whom?—is submerged under a quantitative view in which brute numbers about gross city product, tax base, property values, average incomes, and population change are seen merely as numbers. That produces a decidedly one-sided view of growth. It means you can average the high income and bonuses of Wall Street financial traders with the level of welfare of the unemployed, see the low wages of jobs that attract immigrants as an unproblematic good, and view construction of ever higher priced luxury housing as an end in itself.

This one-sided view of growth has consequences that the city's planning processes are constituted to deal with. But planning designed to deal with those consequences is being systematically sabotaged. The consequence is that the full resources of the city of New York are being channeled into one sector of the economy: the financial sector. It is that sector that is portrayed as the "motor of the city's economy" and the motor of its desirable growth. The net result is that Wall Street, more specifically Lower Manhattan, becomes the ultimate target and beneficiary of all development and growth; anywhere else is encouraged to the extent it feeds into that sector.

The result is growing income inequality, growing luxury housing and declining affordable housing, jobs dependent on financial cycles and crises, amenities oriented to the wealthy, and an educational system steadily underfunded and narrowed in purpose. It doesn't have to be that way.

The nature and direction of growth is a matter very much subject to public control. Government plays a crucial role in economic growth and development and always has. And government actions are, at least in theory, subject to popular, democratic control. Certainly in New York City, of all places, the long-fought battles for the steadily increasing ability of its residents to participate in—and mold—the city's direction is a proud part of the city's history. It is a history that travels from the days of the political bosses and the open rule of the power elite towards fairer elections and the era of more democratic representation in its governing bodies.

On planning matters, the power of the bosses was reduced by the establishment of the New Deal of the City Planning Commission. Community planning boards were established all over the city in 1963 and converted to community boards in 1975 with powers not only to influence planning but also to oversee and influence the management of city services in a decentralized and democratic process. On paper, for a city the size of New York City, it is a very respectable model of how democratic planning can be. For example, the recent discussion of the fate of the World Trade Center site after 9/11 produced a planning review session held at the Convention Center with more than 5,000 people, with participants linked by computers to a scoring system reflecting the majority opinion on a variety of key questions.

But the formal procedures are deceptive. They can be used to implement democracy, or to cover unilateral decisions, made from the top down, with a veneer of depoliticized consent. For it is the political content of these processes, not their form, that counts. Look at the history of the past few years: The most striking example is the so-called PlanNYC2030, often referred to as a long-term master plan for the city's future. But it starts out with a prediction of major growth, in population terms from 8.2 million in 2000 to more than 9 million residents by 2030, simply as an unjustified straight-line extension of past population growth. The whole plan is geared to that growth, making the prediction, in effect, a hoped-for, self-fulfilling prophesy.

Based on that prediction, the plan is for the necessary infrastructure to accommodate it, and in particular to make it available to the service of the financial sector and the business interests of Lower Manhattan. Transportation improvements are directed towards getting people in and out of that area, a direct link for international businessmen from JFK Airport to lower Manhattan is proposed, the necessary water supply and utilities for the additional population is prescribed. And the inevitable environmental consequences of this growth are confronted and dealt with, so that the city will remain green despite the increased load on its physical structure created by this growth.

The questions that ought to be examined in such a plan—but are, in fact, ignored—are legion. What is the relation of population growth to "economic growth?" What are the alternate forms of economic growth that could be considered? Who benefits and who pays for each of the different alternatives? What are the implications for education, for affordable housing, for the range of jobs foreseen, for health care, for public safety, for democratic public spaces (not just for "breathing room" in the crowded city)? Will the polarization of the city be increased or decreased by what is proposed? Will poverty increase, or decrease? Will segregation by race increase, or decrease? Will women be better off than before, or worse off? A "master plan," indeed, but for a narrow segment of the population, a very one-sided plan likely to produce disproportionate benefits for very different population groups in the city.

Did the citizenry, through the city's democratic planning processes, approve this plan? No. They were not asked. The plan was prepared by the deputy mayor for economic development, in an Office for Sustainable Development (with no reference of to whom it is sustainable). The City Planning Commission, responsible for planning under the City Charter, was consulted for occasional technical assistance, no more. The Community Boards were totally ignored, replaced by administratively-convened public hearings, and even their results carried little weight and had not legal force or effect.

A wide range of decisions related to the organization of the city reflect the same pattern of decisions made with a one-sided view of the desirable direction of the city's growth. Gentrification is encouraged by rezoning, which make desirable locations available to the workers and managers of the financial services industry. Money is allocated to improve transportation near the Manhattan business core, and bus service in its residential neighborhoods is left untended and unimproved. Affordable housing is made dependent on the construction of unaffordable housing, with bonuses given to the unaffordable if a little affordable is included. Areas suitable for industrial expansion are rezoned for commercial and residential uses, although the beneficiaries of the one are very different from the beneficiaries of the other. Even such a site as the World Trade Center is developed with a view to its attraction to tourists and its capability to provide office space for international exchange, with cultural concerns taking third place after business and tourism, and affordable housing not even considered.[1]

The solution is not very complicated, at least in theory: reinvigorate and expand the democratic component of the city's planning process, and let the citizenry decide among the alternatives available for its future. Tom Angotti, in a recent book tellingly entitled *New York for Sale*, speaks of community planning as a key component, strengthening the capacity and the formal power of the communities of the city in its over-all planning.[2]

The answer is a political one. Jane Jacobs found that out years ago battling urban renewal and slum clearance programs in Lower Manhattan; her book, *Death and Life of Great American Cities*, was powerful not only for its formulation of new insights but also because it became a weapon in a political struggle. The defeat of Robert Moses' most outrageous proposals for the restructuring of New York in the interests of unlimited growth is another example of the political process working effectively in the public interest. Reinvigorating the tools we already have, and using them in an organized and informed political process to restore democratic control to the planning of the city, is what is needed if economic growth, along with growth generally, is to serve the interests of the majority of New Yorkers, with liberty and justice for all.

The best recipe for economic growth that serves the interests of the majority, not just the elite, is a democratic process for making the decisions that play a role in determining that growth. Implementing a democratic planning process can be a major step in that direction.

Peter Marcuse *is Professor Emeritus of Planning in the School of Architecture, Planning and Preservation at Columbia University.*

Endnotes

1   That story is told in Michael Sorkin, *After the World Trade Center* (New York: Routledge, 2002).

2   Robert Fitch had traced the shifting power constellations in the planning of New York City in an earlier book, *The Assassination of New York* (New York: Verso, 1996), and detailed documentation is not hard to come by.

A CASE FOR A PRO-WORKER GROWTH AGENDA

By Peter Ward

A s we cope with an immense economic crisis, the depths of which we still do not know, many people are trying to use the situation to pursue an anti-union agenda. They make the argument that unions are one of the problems we need to fix in order to get out of this fiscal crisis. In fact, the opposite is true. If we want the crisis, both nationally and locally, to be as short and shallow as possible, we should be encouraging workers to join unions, fixing labor laws to allow workers to freely choose whether or not to join a union and implementing economic development policies that support unionized industries that pay decent wages.

Unions are one of the reasons we historically have had a middle class in this country. According to American Rights at Work, a nonprofit labor advocacy organization, union workers earn 30 percent more than non-union workers in the same industry. And nearly 80 percent of unionized workers get employer-sponsored health care. Only 49 percent of non-union workers get those kinds of benefits.[1]

Historically, unions helped raise the wages of non-union workers as well, since non-union employers had to compete with union employers for workers. This impact of unions has declined as union density dropped 30 percent-plus, reaching 7.4 percent of the private sector in 2006. (It is important to note that this drop has occurred despite the fact that 53 percent of workers say they want union representation.[2])

The decline of union density over the last 30 years is one of the reasons that income inequality has widened so dramatically. According to a December 2007 analysis of Congressional Budget Office data by the Center on Budget and Policy Priorities, income inequality in 2005 was at the highest level since 1929.[3] One of the reasons for this is that workers' wages have not increased along with productivity. While productivity increased 20 percent from 2001 to 2006, real wages only went up 2 percent.[4] When workplaces are unionized, workers are much more likely to see wages rise with productivity.

To see the importance of union representation and, in particular, union density—the percentage of workers who are a part of labor groups—for raising basic quality of life standards, one need only look at how hotel workers fare around the country. As with most other jobs, union density is extremely low in the hospitality sector nationwide. Throughout the United States, working in a hotel is a low-wage job with poor working conditions.

Even in major hospitality markets, such as Miami and Houston, where union density is low (less than 20 percent) the vast majority of hotel workers earn wages in the $7–8/hour range, with little if any benefits. However, where union density is higher, workers have been able to achieve significant improvements. Where union density is around 50 percent (such as in Boston and Chicago), hotel wages start at $10–12/hour and employers offer reasonable health care and retirement plans. Union density is highest in New York City and San Francisco, in the 70–80 percent range. Hotel workers in those cities are able to earn middle class incomes, with wages starting at $18–20/hour, high-quality healthcare, and defined-benefit pension plans.

New York City is experiencing an unprecedented wave of hotel development. In 2006, there were roughly 250 hotels in the five boroughs, totaling approximately 90,000 rooms. About 75 percent of those rooms are in unionized hotels. A sustained period of record performance has resulted in more than 240 proposed new hotels, a development pipeline of 30,000 rooms. The vast majority of these projects are being undertaken by developers who are new to New York City and take it for granted that hotels will operate non-union.

The majority of new hotels are limited service establishments, offering no food and beverage and minimal individual service to guests. Workers at these hotels often earn wages in the $8–10/hour range with limited or unaffordable benefits: less than half what their union counterparts make on the same block, but on par with workers in cities where the cost of living is substantially lower. These employers tend to be virulently anti-union, opposing workers' organizing efforts just as repressively as they do elsewhere.

In fact, the emergence of this second-tier industry contains within it the seeds of a potentially permanent decline in wage and benefit standards for hotel workers in New York City. If new hotels are completed in the next few years, and virtually all of them are non-union, Hotel Trades Council could see its density fall from 75 % in 2006 to 61 % in 2012, making bargaining much more difficult. Without policy changes at the local, state and national level, a sector of the economy that provides stable, middle-class jobs could become a sector of the economy that creates exploitative, low-wage jobs instead.

If you listen carefully, you can hear a steady drumbeat of anti-union rhetoric disguised as solutions to the economic crisis. Unionized workers who have fought hard over the years to negotiate decent wages and benefits are being blamed for the economic crisis. Take the example of the United Auto Workers and the automobile industry.

As the rescue of the auto industry was being discussed, General Motors' vice chairman said this about the UAW to *The New York Times*:

> "You get these people who say, 'I know what I'd do if I were C.E.O. of G.M., like close up all the union plants and set up plants down South with non-union labor,' " he said. "Well, any idiot can figure that one out. But how conceivably can you get that done?" [5]

There are two problems with this argument. The first is that the wages and benefits that the Big Three pay are not the cause of their problems. Labor costs only make up about 10 % of the cost of a Big Three car. And the most significant difference between the wage and benefits that the Big Three pay and those of the "transplants" are that the Big Three have a lot of retirees for whom they are paying health care and pensions.[6]

But here's the bigger problem. If taken to its logical extreme, this argument makes it sound like solving this economic crisis requires workers to be paid poverty wages and forgo health care. This point of view is symptomatic of a grave misunderstanding of the purpose of government assistance in economic recovery: to avert an explosion of poverty, homelessness, and Depression-era suffering for millions of people.

The effort to exploit the financial crisis essentially to depress wages is not just immoral, it is also economically counterproductive. As wages go down, consumption will drop even further, hurting the economy even more.

Instead of decreasing wages, we need to figure out how to keep wages and benefits up during the downturn, which, among other things, means supporting unions and workers' desires to join a union. We need to re-create the virtuous cycle of the post-war era, when productivity, wages and consumption were all increasing.

To that end, here are some possible steps we can take to help ensure that workers have the wages and benefits they need to put our economy on the right track.

Locally, we should focus on creating jobs in industries that pay well—not just the hospitality industry but also in manufacturing, construction and other service sectors. This means reducing our reliance on economic development programs, such as Empire Zones and the Industrial and Commercial Abatement Program, programs that benefit companies regardless of the type or quality of job they create. It is counterproductive for tax breaks and other assistance to go to companies that don't create any jobs, or that create jobs that pay poverty or near-poverty wages. Instead, we should target economic development to unionized industries and other industries that pay decent wages.

New York should invest in green infrastructure on an even larger scale than what is envisioned in the Bloomberg administration's much-celebrated PlaNYC. Such an effort could retool and diversify the city's economy in an equitable, forward-thinking fashion, simultaneously making the city more livable and preserving its status as a world leader in economic innovation and urban development. Visionary programs like the Milwaukee Energy Efficiency (Me2) model for retrofitting existing residential and commercial buildings could create tens of thousands of quality construction and manufacturing jobs in skilled trades and emerging industries, while decreasing energy costs and making substantial improvements in air quality and carbon emissions.

Peter Ward *is president of the New York Hotel & Motel Trades Council, AFL-CIO.*

Endnotes

1   http://www.americanrightsatwork.org/component/option,com_issues/Itemid,366/view,issue/id,12/.

2   Richard B. Freeman, "Do Workers Still Want Unions? More Than Ever," Economic Policy Institute, Washington, D.C. (2007), p.6.

3   "Income Inequality Hits Record Levels, New CBO Data Show: Incomes Rose $180,000 for Top 1 Percent in 2005 But Just $400 for Middle-Income Households." By Arloc Sherman. December 17, 2007.

4   "Unions, the economy, and employee free choice." Harley Shaiken.

5   "G.M., Under Pressure, Turns to Robert Lutz." Bill Vlasic. *NY Times*. December 9, 2008. Page B1.

6   Economic Scene: $73 an Hour: Adding It Up." David Leonhardt. *NY Times*. December 10, 2008. Page A1.

SALVAGING THE STIMULUS
By Harry Moroz

T he enactment of the American Recovery and Reinvestment Act of 2009 ended a highly partisan debate in Congress that reverberated throughout the country. While opponents criticized the stimulus as representing bloated, wasteful spending, it was largely greeted by others—New Yorkers foremost among them—as critical, landmark legislation, desperately needed to create new jobs.

Without question, the funds New York City will receive from the stimulus package—between $4 billion and $5 billion—represent an extraordinary investment by the federal government in the nation's most important city. Since Gerald Ford's presidency a generation ago, Washington has, with few exceptions, ignored urban areas. Between 1977 and 2000, for example, federal aid to cities dropped 59.4 percent.[1] Yet, despite the enthusiasm by which it was greeted by many New Yorkers, the stimulus package's sizeable investment does not yet mark a shift in how the federal government treats cities. In fact, the stimulus is even at risk of failing in New York if certain adjustments are not made.

In short, the stimulus has placed on local government agencies the burden of spending effectively and, at the same time, chronicling those efficiencies in ways they have never before had to detail. What's more, there is a growing concern that the funds from the stimulus are being allocated in a manner that benefits politicians as much as the people they seek to represent.

Since virtually the moment the act was passed, New York City and New York State have emphasized transparency and accountability as the keys to the success of the stimulus. Transparency and accountability, it was reasoned, would help prevent waste and abuse and ensure that the best projects—those that create the most jobs most quickly and that establish the foundations for long-term economic recovery—are undertaken. To this end, Governor David A. Paterson created an Economic Recovery and Reinvestment Cabinet, which is in charge of distributing much of New York's $27 billion share of stimulus funds. Meanwhile, Mayor Michael R. Bloomberg launched Stimulus Tracker, a website complete with interactive maps and detailed descriptions of the progress of individual projects.

Despite all that, a lack of coordination between the federal government and cities like New York threatens to undermine efforts at transparency and accountability. First, federal guidelines for tracking the stimulus do not (at least initially) require reporting of how stimulus funds are ultimately used or if they are passed from a state government to a local government and on to another organization like a contractor.[2] Furthermore, cities already face budget shortfalls that are leading to cuts of oversight staff at the very time that these personnel are most needed. The Department of Investigation, New York City's independent government watchdog, reduced its budget by 8 percent in the 2009 fiscal year. And it foresees another 8 percent cut for the following fiscal year, when it will employ just half as many staffers as it did in 2002.[3] Though Congress has introduced legislation to help fund such staff, the Recovery Act does not include money for this purpose and additional oversight spending is unlikely to garner enough congressional support for passage. Indeed, after years of federal disinvestment from cities, the staff that remains is generally unaccustomed to expending large sums of federal money and certainly has never before been expected to expend so much so quickly.

Finally, city agencies face a difficult challenge in determining the impact, and thus evaluating the success, of the stimulus package. For instance, Timothy Gilchrist, the chairman of the Recovery Cabinet, has expressed concern that states, local governments, and other stimulus-fund recipients have not been provided a common set of tools to report the job creating effects of the Recovery Act.[4] Indeed, in announcing $423 million in new federal funding for the New York City Housing Authority, the Mayor emphasized the number of jobs that the funds would create as much as he emphasized the important improvements to public housing that the money has made possible.

One wonders how effectively NYCHA, normally focused on providing affordable housing, can track the jobs created by its projects.[5]

These problems are particularly worrisome because spending at the local level, in general, and in New York City, in particular, is so important. The Brookings Institution estimates that nearly 43 percent of spending under the Recovery Act will occur in metropolitan areas and it points out that the concentration of people, jobs and economic activity in metropolitan areas "means that any national recovery will be driven substantially by the recovery of U.S. metro areas."[6]

While many observers believed New York City to be immune to the economic crisis as the city's economy outperformed much of the country until late 2008, the Independent Budget Office now warns that the city's economy will "contract more sharply and recover more slowly than the U.S. as a whole."[7] Job losses are expected to total 270,000 with most of these to occur in 2009 and 2010.[8] Total tax revenues will fall by $2.6 billion in fiscal year 2009 and an additional $1.3 billion in the following fiscal year.[9] It currently appears that economic recovery in New York will be more L-shaped than V-shaped: a high unemployment rate will persist, while vital city services that have already been pared will remain at risk of budget cuts. Furthermore, New York City will be forced to wean itself from its overreliance on a booming financial services industry, which is unlikely to return to its former prominence.

Thus, the effectiveness of the stimulus package—its ability to create jobs quickly while investing in medium- and long-term economic recovery—is particularly important to New York City. To make the stimulus work for New York, significant guidance must come from the federal government. The stimulus should serve as an opportunity for the federal government to distance itself from recent history when Washington held cities at arm's length while occasionally bribing them with Community Development Block Grant funds and other sweeteners.

First, the federal government must establish guidelines for the assessment of progress, such as number of jobs created, as Mr. Gilchrist has advised. There is no reason why New York City agencies should learn new modes of assessment from scratch at a time when agency expertise is needed to carry out the very projects best suited to economic recovery. Besides, patchwork assessment schemes in cities and states across the country would make broader evaluations of the stimulus's success extremely difficult. (The inconsistent state standards required by the federal No Child Left Behind law are just one example of the danger of such a conflicting patchwork system.)

But, more importantly, the federal government must make its presence felt in New York City beyond guidelines for assessment and requirements for oversight. Indeed, the notion that federal oversight of city stimulus spending is sufficient relies on an antiquated view of the relationship between cities and the federal government that portrayed Washington doing best for cities when it was doing least.

Instead, the Obama administration should rebuild its formidable political operation as a policy operation. This team of operatives would certainly assist New York City with assessment in such areas as job creation and expenditures. But the team's primary role would be to support project development and implementation, always emphasizing the need for city agencies and officials to think both about short-term job creation and a medium- and long-term economic recovery based on sophisticated infrastructure decisions and strategic investments in areas like green technology, energy retrofits and even the rehabilitation of foreclosed properties into rental housing.

Consider the scene in the New York State capitol building[10] last March: Mr. Gilchrist and the Recovery Cabinet sat in Room 246—the cabinet's "situation room"—pouring over innumerable proposals for spending stimulus dollars and weighing rival priorities alongside federal requirements for timeliness and legitimacy. Now imagine representatives of the Obama White House—staffers for, say, his urban policy chief—inviting representatives of the Metropolitan Transit Authority and New York City and sitting with the New York leaders to establish parameters for stimulus spending. They would clarify the federal requirements and move projects that create sustainable jobs and serve broader interests to the top of the pile. They would think less about the current geographical distribution of stimulus projects and more about the medium- and long-term benefits to New York as a whole, pointing out the broader benefits of investment in New York City. For example, they might focus on coordinating funds to rehab foreclosed properties with funds to improve mass transit service, an effort that would spur growth and development in different areas.

Many stimulus watchers have emphasized the importance of accountability and transparency to ensure that Recovery Act funds are spent appropriately and effectively in New York City. While necessary, this emphasis is insufficient. For accountability and transparency to have significance, the federal government must partner with New York City to guide stimulus spending as it happens. It is not too late for this effort to begin, as much of the spending will occur in 2010 and beyond.

The likelihood of an extended downturn in New York, characterized by high unemployment and low tax revenue, makes efficient expenditure of stimulus funds in the city particularly important. And effective coordination between the federal government, state government, and city officials will help ensure the long-term viability and economic and social benefits of the investment in stimulus funds.

Harry Moroz is a research associate at the Drum Major Institute for Public Policy.

Endnotes

1   See Wallin "Budgeting for Basics: The Changing Landscape of City Finances".

2   See Robinson testimony.

3   http://query.nytimes.com/gst/fullpage.html?res=9500E1DA163EF933A15750C0A96F9C8B63.

4   Gilchrist testimony.

5   See GAO report.

6   Brookings ARRA.

7   Lowenstein testimony.

8   Lowenstein testimony.

9   Lowenstein testimony.

10 http://www.nytimes.com/2009/03/05/nyregion/05albany.html?hp.

EDUCATION AND ECONOMIC OPPORTUNITY

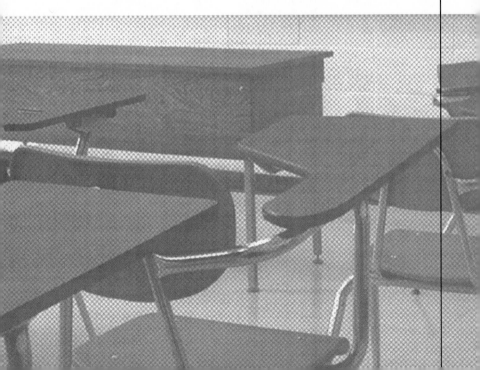

LEVELLING THE SCHOOL PLAYING FIELD: A CRITICAL AIM FOR NEW YORK'S FUTURE

By Richard D. Kahlenberg

I n recent years, the debate over reform of New York City public schools has focused on a number of hot-button issues, from mayoral control and the expansion of charter schools to merit pay for teachers and the role of teacher unions in education. Promising innovative programs, like the Harlem Children's Zone, which provides pre-kindergarten parenting classes and extra social services to low-income students, and the Knowledge is Power Program (KIPP) charter schools, have received a great deal of media attention. But there is one thing that all these approaches have in common: they are committed to the idea of trying to make "separate" schools for rich and poor "equal." In the coming years, if New York City's public schools wish to educate both the middle class and the aspiring middle class to high levels, steps must be taken to reduce the fountainhead of school inequality: severe concentrations of poverty in the public schools.

To date, New York City has had some modest success trying to improve the achievement levels in high-poverty schools. But if school officials want to provide genuine equal opportunity, they need to find creative ways to reduce the separation of low-income, middle-class and affluent students in the city's public schools. New York must and can do better than "separate but equal" schooling.

For 40 years, researchers have found that the single most important predictor of academic achievement is the socioeconomic status of the family from which a child comes. And the second most important predictor is the socioeconomic makeup of the school she attends.[1] All students—rich, poor, white, black, Latino and Asian—perform significantly better in schools with strong middle-class populations than they do in high-poverty schools. Virtually everything that educators talk about as desirable in a school—high standards and expectations, good teachers, active parents, a safe and orderly environment, a stable student and teacher population—are more likely to be found in economically mixed schools than in high-poverty schools.

While it is possible to make schools with high concentrations of poverty work—we all know of achievements within selected schools—it is extremely uncommon. For example, a study by Douglas Harris, a professor at the University of Wisconsin, found that middle-class schools (those with fewer than 50 percent of students eligible for free and reduced-price lunches) are 22 times more likely to be consistently high performing as high-poverty schools (those with 50 percent or more of students eligible for subsidized lunches.)[2]

Middle-class schools perform better in part because their students, on average, receive more support at home and come to school better prepared. But the vastly different educational environments typically found in middle-class and high-poverty schools also have a profound effect on achievement. On the 2007 National Assessment of Educational Progress exam given to fourth graders in math, for example, low-income students attending more affluent schools scored substantially higher (241) than low-income students in high-poverty schools (221). This 20-point difference is the equivalent of almost two year's learning. Indeed, low-income students given a chance to attend more affluent schools performed more than half a year better, on average, than middle-income students who attend high-poverty schools (232).[3] At the high school level, similar results are found. In 2005, for example, University of California professor Russell Rumberger and his colleague, Gregory J. Palardy, found that a school's socioeconomic status had as much impact on the achievement growth of high school students as a student's individual economic status.[4]

Why does it matter to student achievement if a child attends a middle class or high-poverty school? While money matters a great deal in education, people matter more. Consider the three main sets of actors in a school: students, parents, and faculty (teachers and principals). Research suggests that students learn a great deal from their peers, so it is an advantage to have classmates who are academically engaged and aspire to go on to college. Peers in middle-income schools are more likely to do homework and graduate, an less likely to watch television and cut class—all of which have been found to influence the behavior of classmates. Middle-class schools report disorder problems half as often as low-income schools, so more learning goes on. It is also an advantage to have high achieving peers, whose knowledge is shared informally with classmates all day long. Middle-class peers come to schools with twice the vocabulary of low-income children, for example, so any given child is more likely to expand his vocabulary in a middle-class school through informal interaction.[5]

Parental involvement also plays a critical role in student success. Thereusive research that strates that it is an advantage for a student to attend a school where parents are actively involved, volunteer in the classroom, and hold school officials accountable. Research repeatedly finds that middle-class parents are more likely to be involved in schools. Not having to work three jobs and having a car makes it easier for middle-class parents to be involved. So, it's not surprising that in middle-class schools parents are four times as likely to be members of the Parent Teacher Association.[6]

Finally, research finds that the best teachers, on average, are attracted to middle-class schools. Teachers in middle-class schools are more likely to be licensed, to teach in their field of expertise, to have high teacher test scores, to have more teaching experience, and to have more formal education. Teachers generally consider it a promotion to move from poor to middle class schools and many of the best teachers transfer into middle-income schools at their first opportunity. Moreover, teachers in middle-class schools are more likely to have high expectations. Research has found that the grade of C in a middle-income school is the same as a grade of A in a low-income school, as measured by standardized tests results. Middle-class schools are also more likely to offer advanced placement classes and high-level math courses.[7]

Significantly, studies find that middle-class children are not hurt academically by attending economically mixed schools. The research suggests that sprinkling a few middle-class kids into a school of highly concentrated poverty might hurt their academic achievement, but so long as a majority of the students are middle class (not eligible for free and reduced price lunch), middle-class student achievement does not decline with the presence of some low-income students. Studies find that integration is not a zero sum game;, in whcor low-income students are not offset by declines in middle-class achievement. This is true in part because the majority sets the tone in a school, and bcause research finds that middle-class children are less affected by school influences (for good or ill) than low-income children.[8]

Today, more than 60 districts are pursuing policies of socioeconomic school integration, breaking up concentrations of poverty and giving all students a chance to attend economically mixed schools. The list includes districts from both "red" states and "blue" states, districts that are urban and suburban, southern, northern, eastern and western: from Wake County (Raleigh), N.C., to San Francisco, Calif.; from La Crosse, Wisc., to Cambridge, Mass.; from St. Lucie County, Fla., to Rochester, N.Y., to McKinney, Texas.

School districts have learned a great deal about how to integrate students with different backgrounds since the crisis over busing in the 1970s. Today, most districts rely primarily on systems of magnet schools and public school choice, rather than compulsory busing, to achieve their goal of socioeconomic integration. In Cambridge, for example, all schools have been designated magnet schools. Parents rank their preferences among schools and the district honors choices in a way to ensure that all schools are within plus or minus 10 percentage points of the system's average eligibility for free and reduced price lunch.

While most economic integration programs are fairly new, the early results are promising. In Wake County, for example, there is an extensive system of magnet schools in the city of Raleigh. Having those schools in place helps the district reach toward its goal that no school have more than 40 percent of its students eligible for free and reduced-price lunch or more than 25 percent reading below grade level. According to Gerald Grant's important new book, *Hope and Despair in the American City: Why There are No Bad Schools in Raleigh*, Wake County's efforts "reduced the gap between rich and poor, black and white, more than any other large urban educational system in America."[9]

How would a program like this work in New York City, where the system overall has fairly high levels of poverty? District-wide, roughly three quarters of New York City public school elementary school students are eligible for free or reduced-price school lunches.[10]

An evenstribution of low-income students across all New York City public schools would leave all with relatively high levels of poverty, an undesirable outcome. Instead, New York City public schools need to take four steps to increase the number of high quality economically integrated public schools.

First, New York City should seek to create additional theme-based schools that will draw more middle- and upper-middle-class students back into the public school system. New York City currently has a fairly high percentage of students using private school. At the high school level, 18 percent of students use private school, the second highest share among the top 10 largest American cities.[11] Althoughew York City currently has an extensive public school choice program in place, it could be enhanced with careful polling of private school parents to determine what it would take to attract their children back into the public school system. What sort of pedagogical and thematic offerings would they find to be enticing? Over the past seven years, New York City has opened hundreds of new schools, according to the New York City Public Schools Office of Portfolio Planning.[12] If that tnd continues, there will be ample opportunity to strengthen the New York City public schools for everyone by enrolling a broader cross section of New York City school-aged children.

One particularly promising strategy is to form partnerships between individual public schools and New York City's many prestigious institutions: Yankee Stadium, the Museum of Natural History, the New York Public Library, Lincoln Center, New York University, Columbia Presbyterian Hospital, Broadway theaters, Wall Street institutions and others. The notion here is not that 20 schools conduct an annual tour of the Metropolitan Museum of Art, but rather that an individual school would form a close partnership with the museum, in which docents would meet with school children regularly to expose them to a special arts curriculum.

Over time, these schools of choice would develop annual data on their popularity. Certain schools are likely to be over-chosen time and time again, while others will be under-chosen. As school consultants Michael Alves and Charles Willie have written, under-chosen schools should be closed and reopened with more popular themes, while over-chosen schools can be franchised. For example, in Cambridge, which has a system of universal choice and seeks an economic balance among schools, officials recently turned the struggling predominantly low-income Tobin school, located near a large low-income housing complex, into a Montessori. In the 2006–07 school year, Tobin had attracted only 12 first-choice applicants to fill 60 pre-kindergarten and kindergarten seats. The next year, when it reopened as a Montessori, Tobin attracted 145 applicants, with twice as many middle-class as low-income students applying, according to Alves, who administers the student lottery.

Second, to create a more economically mixed student population into the New York City public schools, the system could create partnerships with more affluent suburban jurisdictions neighboring city schools. As Amy Stuart Wells of Teachers College, Columbia University and Jennifer Jellison Holme of the University of Texas at Austin explain, long-standing inter-district integration programs exist in eight communities—Boston; East Palo Alto, Calif.; Hartford, Conn.; Indianapolis; Milwaukee; Minneapolis; Rochester, N.Y.; and St. Louis. These programs, which provide the opportunity for low-income minority students to transfer to better performing suburban schools, while also often providing magnet school programs to draw in suburban students, have generally produced very positive outcomes for students.[13] In Hartford, for example, many urban children have benefitted from the opportunity to attend high achieving suburban schools, while there are long waiting lists of white middle-class students for urban magnets with themes like Multiple Intelligences and Montessori programs.[14]

Third, to ensure that magnet programs do not create small enclaves of privilege within New York City's public schools, the district should take steps to ensure that the new influx of middle-class children benefits all students in the system. Although the United States Supreme Court now disfavors the use of race in promoting school integration, it is perfectly legal to look at socioeconomic status, which we noted earlier is the key factor in raising student achievement. In honoring choices among public schools, New York City school officials can consider factors such as eligibility for subsidized lunch to ensure that choice is promoting socioeconomically integrated student bodies. In fact, for several years, two consortia of magnet school programs in Brooklyn have been considered free and reduced eligibility in honoring choices to oversubscribed programs; and this consideration could be greatly expanded throughout the system.[15]

For selective schools, such as Stuyvesant or the Bronx School of Science, New York City could consider test scores in the context of economic obstacles that a student has overcome. Public opinion polling has long found that while there is roughly 2-to-1 opposition to using racial preferences in admissions to selective educational institutions, there is 2-to-1 support for giving a preference to low income students of all races.[16]

Charter schools, a growing sector of New York City's public school system, could likewise consider socioeconomic diversity as a factor in admitting students to oversubscribed schools. There is some evidence that on a national level, charter schools are actually increasing segregation of students by socioeconomic status and race.[17] However, as schools of choice, which decouple the link between schools and residential segregation, charter schools have the potential to promote greater integration.

Fourth, in developing new public and charter school buildings, New York City should systematically seek to enhance economic integration by locating facilities in a way that draws upon diverse student pools. Instead of building a school in either a highly wealthy or a highly poor area, new schools could be placed on the boundaries of wealthy and poor areas, so as to draw upon both sets of populations.

Richard D. Kahlenberg, a senior fellow at The Century Foundation, is author of All Together Now: Creating Middle-Class Schools through Public School Choice; *and* Tough Liberal: Albert Shanker and the Battles Over Schools, Unions, Race and Democracy, *newly out in paperback.*

Endnotes

1 See James S. Coleman, et al, *Equality of Educational Opportunity* (Washington D.C.: U.S. Government Printing Office, 1966). The basic findings of the report have been affirmed again and again in the research literature. See Richard D. Kahlenberg, *All Together Now: Creating Middle-Class Schools through Public School Choice* (Washington D.C.: Brookings Institution Press, 2001), pp. 25-35 (reviewing numerous studies.)

2 Douglas N. Harris, "Ending the Blame Game on Educational Inequity: A Study of 'High Flying' Schools and NCLB," Education Policy Research Unit, Arizona State University, March 2006.

3 National Center of Education Statistics, NAEP Data Explorer, 2008.

4 R.W. Rumberger, and G. J. Palardy, "Does Segregation Still Matter? The Impact of Student Composition on Academic Achievement in High School" *Teachers College Record*, Vol 107, No. 9, 1999-2045 (2005).

5 Kahlenberg, *All Together Now*, pp. 50-58.

6 Kahlenberg, *All Together Now*, pp. 62-64.

7 Kahlenberg, *All Together Now*, pp. 67-74.

8 Kahlenberg, *All Together Now*, pp. 37-42.

9 Gerald Grant, *Hope and Despair in the American City: Why There are No Bad Schools in Raleigh* (Cambridge, MA: Harvard University Press, 2009), p. 92.

10 New York State Kids' Well-being Indicators Clearinghouse, "Children Receiving Free or Reduced-Price School Lunch—Public Schools, grades K-6, 2007-08" available at http://www.nyskwic.org/access_data/ind_profile.cfm?subIndicatorID=52.

11 William Sander, "Private schools and school enrollment in Chicago," Chicago Fed Letter, The Federal Reserve Bank of Chicago, October 2006, p. 1.

12 New York City Public Schools, "New District Schools," available at http://schools.nyc.gov/community/planning/newschools/default.htm.

13 Jennifer Jellison Holme and Amy Stuart Wells, "School Choice Beyond District Borders: Lessons for Reauthorization of NCLB through Interdistrict Desegregation and Open Enrollment Programs," in Richard D. Kahlenberg (ed), *Improving on No Child Left Behind: Getting Education Reform Back on Track* (New York: Century Foundation Press, 2008).

14 Richard D. Kahlenberg, "The New Brown: Integration by Class, Not Race, Can Fix Schools in Poor Cities," *Legal Affairs*, May 2003, available at http://www.legalaffairs.org/printerfriendly.msp?id=380.

15 See Richard D. Kahlenberg, "Rescuing Brown v. Board of Education: Profiles of Twelve Districts Pursuing Socioeconomic Integration through Public School Choice" (2007), p. 46 n.21, available at http://www.tcf.org/publications/education/districtprofiles.pdf.

16 See Richard D. Kahlenberg, "Introduction," in Richard D. Kahlenberg (ed), *America's Untapped Resource: Low-Income Students in Higher Education* (New York: Century Foundation Press, 2004), p. 14 (citing 2003 polls from *Newsweek* and the *Los Angeles Times*).

17 See Erica Frankenberg & Genevieve Siegel-Hawley, "The Forgotten Choice? Rethinking Magnet Schools in a Changing Landscape," Civil Rights Project at UCLA, November 2008, p. 15.

MAKING NEW YORK CITY FLOURISH: INVEST IN COMMUNITY COLLEGES

By Gail O. Mellow

A century ago, higher education in New York City looked very different from today. It reflected the needs of the nation's largest city, an industrial and commercial behemoth, which required millions of men and women to work in its shipyards, sugar refineries, and garment factories. At the beginning of the 20th Century, few adults attended one of the many colleges or universities in New York City. Higher education was for an elite few, educating a tiny minority of the city's population. College students then were financially well-off white males who would assume top level jobs in the city's small "white collar" economy: the corporate, banking and legal sectors.

One hundred years later, our economy, our higher education system, and the needs of our city's residents for higher education look very different. With the advent of what has been termed the "Knowledge Era" or the "Innovation Economy," a college education is more important than ever. In this economy, people must be highly educated to be both productively employed and to participate meaningfully in their communities. The challenge this presents is profound. In order for people to thrive, and for our city to flourish, higher education has to do a better job in enrolling larger numbers of students, closing achievement gaps between sub-populations and having more students completing a degree or certificate. Disturbing educational disparities still exist: African-American and Latino New Yorkers continue to be underrepresented in the population of high school students attending colleges, and males in general are becoming an endangered species at our colleges. Colleges and universities must learn to not only effectively educate every student who graduates from high school but must succeed with a significantly larger swath of the adult population as well.

Unfortunately, we have been hobbled by an unrealistic, almost romantic, version of what the college experience looks like for Americans. The picture of who goes to college has not caught up with the reality of the college-going student of today. Popular media represents a reality that is most germane to a small group of middle- and upper-class parents and students. Look at, for instance, how the "college theme" develops over the year in any magazine or newspaper. It begins in November with high school students taking the SAT tests, continues in the early spring with the nail-biting anxiety of waiting for acceptance into the best schools, and reaches a conclusion in September with images of parents helping their child move into dorms. It just happens to be only a very, very small part of what is actually occurring to the individuals who will be the majority of students in colleges in this city and across the nation.

The reality: Nearly half of all undergraduates, and more than 50 percent of all black and Latino students, attend community colleges. The average American college student, whether attending a two- or four-year college, is over 24 years of age and commutes to college, rather than residing in a dorm. The average student also works, often full time, but typically more than 20 hours per week.

The average American student no longer corresponds to a traditional stereotype of "college student." It is important that policymakers not ignore the vast number of Americans, especially new immigrant, minority and urban students, who don't complete high school in their teens and will return to college later in life. It is essential to appreciate the large number of high school graduates who do graduate, but need intensive remedial help in math, writing, and reading and are not fully ready to take on a full load of college-level courses. We need to recognize that today's college students are very likely to need classes offered in the evening and on weekends to accommodate work schedules and on-campus child care services to allow them to fully concentrate on their studies.

Our city and the nation's higher education policy need to be grounded in the reality of today's college students and today's changing economy. Yet policy change cannot come soon enough because the implications of a narrow, ill-organized higher education system are profound for both individuals and the broader society.

For earlier generations, a high school or GED diploma was sufficient to securing a living wage job. No longer. Completion of a two-year degree has a profound impact on an individual's earning ability and their ability to get and hold a job. According to a 2007 College Board study, median lifetime earnings for individuals with associate degrees from a community college are 28 percent higher than lifetime earnings for those with just a high school degree, and that gap is increasing over time. Higher education is correlated with more stable employment, better health, and superior educational outcomes for the children of parents who attend college.

As a nation, the economy demands better educated and trained workers. Yet, if current trends persist, tomorrow's workforce will be less, not more, educated. Because younger age groups in the nation are more racially and ethnically diverse and have historically lower rates of higher education enrollment and completion, the educational preparedness of Americans will be lower at just the time when we need a more highly educated workforce. This is occurring right at the time when the fastest growing jobs, those that pay a living wage, require a postsecondary education.

Unfortunately, America can no longer sit contently thinking we have the best educated workforce in the world. When the Organization of Economic Cooperation and Development, a group of the 30 wealthiest nations in the world, measures the percentage of adults with at least an associate's degree, we rank 8th. Shockingly, the United States is the only nation within the OECD whose older generation (those between the ages of 45–54) is more educated than those of younger generations (ages 25–34).

The answer to redressing these challenges lies with community colleges. The nation's more than 1,200 community colleges, and the six community colleges of The City University of New York, are a unique system that is best-positioned to meet and fulfill a diverse student body's needs and aspirations. Community colleges have an open admissions policy and accept all students who have earned a high school degree or GED. Sadly, many students—more than 75 percent—are not prepared for college-level work and need remedial help in mathematics, writing or reading. And, despite these challenges, community colleges succeed at providing a brighter future. The extraordinary thing is that community colleges are successful with the students who by any statistical category, such as race, ethnicity, lack of academic preparedness, poverty, or immigration status are not only the most challenging to serve but the least likely to succeed in college. Community colleges also provide GED preparation and extensive English as a Second Language programs to place students on a track towards climbing a career ladder and, for many, a college education.

Community colleges create these miracles while being the least funded sector of education, with fewer dollars than are spent on elementary school students. Our nation's focus on the traditional college-going population has contributed to a severe disparity in support for community colleges. National expenditures for public two-year colleges in 2004 were $24.4 billion. This is less than 20 percent of the $124.8 billion expended by *public* four-year colleges and universities. The gap is shocking. American community colleges, despite enrolling almost half of all undergraduate students, spend 80 percent less than their public four-year sisters. If we looked at it through the lens of per capita spending, we in America spend three times more to educate each four-year college student than we do for a community college student ($27,973 vs. $9,183). Those most prepared to attend college are receiving support at rates far above those who need the highest level of support.

There has finally been a long-sought transformation in the recognition of the invaluable role that community colleges can play in changing lives. In his first address to Congress, President Obama underlined the importance of community colleges when he called upon all Americans to get more education or career training beyond high school. And then, in July 2009, the President laid out an ambitious agenda that would provide $12 billion over five years to the nation's community colleges. The American Graduation Initiative set a national goal of graduating five million more students from community colleges by 2020 as part of a larger goal to restore the United States as the country with the highest college graduation rate.

The President's initiative provides historic support for community colleges, creating for the first time a dedicated federal funding stream for two-year colleges. The proposal, now under consideration by Congress, establishes separate competitive funding processes for states and community colleges to design and implement programs that help students stay in college and complete their studies. To address the intense demand for new classrooms and laboratories, funding would also be available to build new facilities and renovate and modernize older buildings. In addition, the measure provides funding for the development of free high-quality online courses and supports the development of data collection and research efforts to evaluate community college success.

But the banks are standing in the way of progress. Their lobby is quietly pushing Congress to oppose the legislation that would result in enhanced student financial aid and more funding for community colleges. Though it passed the House, special interests have it bottled up in the Senate. Incredible, isn't it? The very same industry that has gotten billions of dollars in bailout money from the federal government is not ready to loosen its grip on the cash cow that is the private student loan industry.

Here in New York City, Mayor Michael R. Bloomberg also stepped up to the plate to underline his support for community colleges. In August 2009, he set a goal of graduating 120,000 New Yorkers from community colleges by 2020 and providing $50 million over the next four years. The mayor's initiative seeks to expand community college education programs by providing funding to increase education and training in nursing and green jobs, to expand the successful Accelerated Study in Associate Program (ASAP), which helps students complete their studies within three years, and to open a new community college in Manhattan. It seeks to build on the strength of community colleges in providing technical support to local businesses by allocating funds to allow the six City University of New York community colleges to provide small business development courses to new entrepreneurs. It helps students stay in school by investing in student advisement services, expanding child care offerings, and reducing the cost of textbooks.

In the philanthropic community there has been a burst of interest and investment by some of the nation's leading foundations. The Gates Foundation, already well-known for its innovative efforts to reshape K-12 education, is investing millions to improve community college completion rates. The Lumina Foundation, a foundation with a deep commitment to community college success, has spearheaded the development of the Achieving the Dream Initiative, a nationwide effort to employ data to better understand why students fail to complete college and to spur the creation of innovative programs.

These efforts are an important step forward. After years of neglect, community colleges are getting the recognition they deserve and the promise of additional funding. But more is still needed.

To reach the President's goal of having America lead the world in the number of college graduates, we will need to recruit a larger group of adults who should be in college, while investing in the faculty and student supports that will reduce the number of students who fail to graduate. This will require a lessening of funding disparities and an even greater investment of both public and private dollars.

Re-envisioning the American higher education system will not be cheap. At a time of declining revenues and growing deficits, it is a supreme challenge. But, the alternative is far worse. We can ill afford to have adult students hungry and ready for more education and training, wanting to earn a degree or certificate that will allow them to earn more, to be turned away because admissions have been closed. We can not have employers unable to expand, or moving their operations, because they are unable to hire employees who have the analytical and technical skills that today's jobs demand. Educating more students to higher standards than before will require a substantive rethinking of the funding mechanisms and the distribution of dollars in higher education.

Community colleges have been essentially given straw and expected to spin gold. Community colleges are the cornerstone of higher education and provide a gateway for students to well-paying jobs and a bachelor's degree. We have allowed the four-year and community college systems to develop separately and unequally, with tenuous points of integration and inadequate financial support. Higher education funding, and too often the tools for how we measure community college success, are premised on what are now nostalgic memories of traditional-aged, upper-middle class college students. Unless we let go of this myth and realistically face the modern demographics of the American college population—who goes and who should go to college—the relevance and status of the American economy in a competitive, global economy will erode.

Gail O. Mellow is the president of LaGuardia Community College.

SCHOOL SUCCESS AND REVERSING ABSENTEEISM: A KEY TO THE CITY'S FUTURE SUCCESS

By Kim Nauer and Andrew White

E ducational failure on the scale currently considered routine in New York and other cities essentially confounds any attempt to reduce this nation's stubborn disparities of income and wealth. For New York City to thrive, many more young people from poor and working-class families will need to succeed in school, to move into higher education, and join the middle-class workforce. But as we've learned in our research, success in school is rooted in far more than academics.

The years spent in primary school are especially important to children's long-term educational success. Yet, tens of thousands of young New York City children carry the difficulties of their home lives into the classroom, where they intrude on a child's ability to learn and flourish. For many children, problems at home prevent them from attending school regularly.

Public school systems that are incapable of helping families and children deal with such problems cannot ensure that students remain on track through their early school years. Research shows that children who fall behind in elementary school are far more likely to struggle in later years and that they are inclined to abandon school altogether as teens.

In a report entitled "Strengthening Schools by Strengthening Families," published by the Center for New York City Affairs at The New School in late 2008, we wrote that chronic absenteeism in New York City schools begins in the earliest grades and is far more serious than had previously been reported. We found that more than 90,000 children in grades K through 5—roughly 20 percent of the city's elementary school enrollment—missed at least a month of school during the 2007–2008 school year. The problem is even more dramatic in low-income and working-class communities. Overcoming this crisis in absenteeism and educational failure is a major prerequisite to putting thousands of city students back on the path to higher achievement and economic success.

A solid education is essential to creating a strong workforce that fosters a thriving economy and a decent standard of living for New York's residents. According to recent reports by McKinsey & Company and America's Promise Alliance, the damaging impact of underachieving schools on the economy is clear. When comparing economic data and education scores in the United States to those in other countries, the cost of our nation's chronic educational underachievement "is substantially larger than the deep recession the United States is currently experiencing," the McKinsey report states. Similarly, America's Promise Alliance links high dropout rates to lagging economic performance among American cities. As all levels of our government look at the current recession and develop economic recovery policies, plans to improve education must be included.

Our own research found many reasons for high rates of chronic absenteeism. These include child health issues such as asthma, transportation problems (particularly for children with disabilities), and dislocations caused by eviction or the difficulties associated with living in homeless shelters. Other issues of family instability are important such as parental depression or illness, domestic violence, and inadequate food or clothing. Absences are also often associated with a family's language barriers and sometimes with problematic family priorities such as extended family vacations taken during the school year.

The schools themselves bear a high responsibility for attendance, both in terms of devoting attention to the issue and in creating welcoming places where children want to be and that parents respect and value. They also shoulder the duty of making sure that parents, including new immigrants and those who may not have a high degree of education, fully understand the importance of education as a public responsibility. But they also have the responsibility of offering guidance to parents on the issues of health and inadequate resources that often prevent children from attending school in the first place.

Addressing these issues directly, alongside absenteeism, may not only improve students' success in the long-term but also strengthen families and improve the quality of many children's lives. School success also improves lifelong earning potential and increases the probability that a family will move out of poverty and into the middle class.

We found that the large majority of children who are chronically absent live in neighborhoods where they are most likely to live in poverty. In fact, in five school districts in central Brooklyn, northern Manhattan and the South Bronx, fully 30 percent of the children were chronically absent in the 2007-2008 school year, missing more than 10 percent of the school year and often much more.

Yet, not every school in these districts has this problem. Some principals have learned how to reduce absenteeism, using creative strategies to engage students and families. For example, one Bronx school with a large Muslim population hired a Muslim man to sit with students at lunch time when they fasted during Ramadan, so that the students might not feel compelled to skip school altogether. This same school has a strong relationship with a local medical center and is improving treatment for the asthma that is chronic among many of its students.

Other schools are working with community-based organizations to reach out to families, to find resources to help them, or to seek intervention when problems are dire. We found notable efforts ranging from all-inclusive "community schools" with a wide-range of social services to more targeted programs that offer roving social workers to assist with behavior issues or family problems.

Successful schools often benefit from strong relationships with local organizations that provide parent outreach and assistance to families. Family-oriented social services—ranging from help with housing and food to referrals for drug and alcohol treatment—are a valuable complement to a school's academic program and can help improve attendance.

In New York City, community schools have a long history of linking children to social services. And there is strong evidence that community schools, when properly funded and staffed, can engage families that struggle with serious difficulties related to living in poverty and also make significant improvements in the lives of vulnerable children. In a community school, students can receive medical and mental health care as well as high-quality tutoring and after-school programs, cutting down on the amount of time their families must spend going to outside medical and social service appointments.

Full-fledged community schools are lauded nationwide as a method for integrating social services, health care, and other supports into the public education system. They rely on formidable partnerships between public school principals and the leadership of community-based nonprofits, such as the Children's Aid Society in New York. However, this model is expensive and requires substantial square-footage for programs, a resource few principals are willing to give up.

However, a key element of this model can be adapted to help many more schools. In this model, community schools employ a high-level specialist who works alongside the principal to manage social services and other outside programs and relationships for the school. This "community schools director" works for a reliable, trusted nonprofit partner and is responsible for developing and coordinating the school's student and family service programs. These professionals typically have master's degrees in social service or youth development and know the landscape of the neighborhoods where they work. They are also capable of coordinating in-school programs and of expanding them outward by vetting and working with groups and institutions outside of the school.

In our report, we recommend that New York City's Department of Education identify 50 to 100 schools with high rates of chronic absenteeism in high-poverty districts and establish executive-level partnerships with outside organizations to put solutions into action.

The city should require that each school in the target group assess the key factors behind the problem of chronic absenteeism. Principals should have access to outside technical assistance to perform this assessment, whether from the department's own support offices or skilled nonprofit providers. Following the assessment, a principal will have a clear understanding of the types of support required to address the problem. Ideally, the principal should be able to interview and select an appropriate partner organization from among several stable, well-respected nonprofit organizations with different specializations, dozens of which exist in New York City.

Once the partner is selected, a professional from the organization will be brought on board to work inside the school at the right hand of the principal—and alongside the school's top administrators and program staff. Students, families and school staff will benefit not only from targeted coordination with outside agencies and institutions but also from expertise regarding existing funding streams and available services.

Absenteeism in elementary schools is disproportionately a problem in low-income and working class minority communities. It immediately puts students behind their middle class peers. The academic pressures build over time and build quickly. While the reasons behind absenteeism and related issues of child welfare are extremely complex, dedicated principals in New York City have proven that this is a problem that can be addressed with careful attention to underlying causes. New York can learn from them and build a more formidable structure for strengthening schools by strengthening families.

Andrew White is director and *Kim Nauer* is education project director of the Center for New York City Affairs, based at Milano The New School for Management and Urban Policy.

INFRASTRUCTURE AND THE BUILT ENVIRONMENT

A TUNNEL TO ECONOMIC HEALTH

By Jerrold Nadler

New York's growth has always been inextricably tied to its transportation infrastructure. In the 19th Century, the Erie Canal, first, and then the Erie Lackawanna and New York Central Railroads built the state. In the first half of the 20th Century, the New York City subway system enabled the city to expand radically into the outer boroughs. At the same time, the expanding thruways and the systems of bridges and tunnels spawned the growth of the suburbs, further augmenting the city and state's great economic engine.

But in the second half of the 20th Century, New York failed to keep its infrastructure up to date and the city suffered tremendous economic losses and disadvantages as a direct result. We have allowed our bridges, highways and mass transit systems to fall dramatically behind in necessary upkeep and expansion. Indeed, New York is the only major port city in the United States that never built a rail freight tunnel or bridge over or under its river or harbor. Consequently, we are today the only major American city that is totally dependent on trucks for our freight movement.

In the 1970s, when I was a member of the New York State Assembly representing the West Side of Manhattan, I first became acutely aware of the problem of freight movement in the New York region. As I grew to be more deeply involved in the issue, it increasingly dawned on me that freight movement—the transport of goods—was an issue of monumental consequence for all of us in our region. But it was also an issue that barely received consideration by elected officials or the media. Few understood how crucial the issue is to our everyday lives—or its importance to our economic future.

Before long, I came to understand that if we did not take freight movement more seriously, New York City and its environs would become choked by truck traffic and pollution and that the inability of our highway system to handle greater volume of truck traffic would place a lid on economic development. There are some simple truths of the matter: Our roads simply cannot handle the current volume of traffic and certainly not a greatly increased level. Our health is at risk from truck-borne pollution. And with added density of population and congestion will surely come greater delays in bringing goods to markets, delays that will further drive up the cost of consumer products. Furthermore, New York's almost total reliance on trucks for delivering goods is extraordinarily destructive to our roads and bridges—not to mention the toll it takes on the water mains and other infrastructure.

I am convinced that the only solution to this economic and public health disaster-in-the-making is to reduce our dependence on trucks for freight movement by connecting the communities east of the Hudson River—Brooklyn, Queens and Long Island, Westchester, and eastern Connecticut—to the national rail grid. This is why, for more than 30 years, I have advocated for the construction of the Cross Harbor Rail Freight Tunnel connecting Brooklyn to New Jersey. While this critical project has gained momentum in recent years, its original inception long predates me.

The Port Authority of New York and New Jersey was created in 1921 for the purpose of operating the port and improving the rail freight system serving the Port district. New York's distinct geographic separation (via the Hudson river) from the rest of the United States presented a set of challenges. Indeed, it was, and still is, the only major port city in the United States disconnected from the nation's freight rail network. The Port Authority was established specifically to solve that problem by constructing an under-the-harbor rail tunnel for the movement of goods. The first chairman of the Port Authority, Eugenius H. Outerbridge, a prominent manufacturing importer and exporter, called the rail freight tunnel from Bay Ridge to Bayonne the "keystone in the arch of the master plan" of the Port Authority. Nearly 90 years later, this project has finally begun to gain dramatic momentum. After an initial start in 1995, in the administration of Mayor Rudolph W. Giuliani, the "Cross Harbor Freight Movement

Project" was transferred in 2008 to the Port Authority, its rightful patron and an environmental impact statement is now underway.

It has taken a long time to get to this point, but it is now clear that cost, land use and environmental considerations will not allow the New York metropolitan region to merely "build its way" out of its congestion problems by expanding its highway capacity. Since freight does not ride buses or subways (or, incidentally, vote), we must find freight-specific solutions to the problem of moving goods and products efficiently and sustainably.

The inefficiency of our goods-movement system is particularly disturbing in a region that is the single largest consuming market in the country. Roughly 320 million tons of freight enters the New York metropolitan region annually. Trucks move more than 98 percent of this freight. That contrasts with most other American cities, which on average bring in only about 60 percent of their freight by truck. Trucking is the major source of congestion and the source of a host of ensuing problems. Fully 30,000 trucks clog key roads and bridges every day, with each large freight truck equaling the roadway capacity of four passenger vehicles. This problem will get much worse in the coming decades as the volume of freight moving through the region increases—a growth of 80 percent by 2025, according to official estimates.

In essence, congestion fundamentally harms our regional economy, environment, public health, and infrastructure. The lack of rail freight access also creates severe national security vulnerability for this region. Furthermore, because of the lack of a direct connection to America's rail network and various constraints on our highways, bridges, and tunnels, a staggering 93 percent of the region's goods enter through the George Washington Bridge.

Any meaningful resolution of the region's congestion problems cannot be accomplished without serious attention being devoted to freight movement. The only conceivable solution is to revitalize the rail freight system in downstate New York. We must connect our region's rail network to the nation's rail freight system by building a Cross-Harbor Rail Freight Tunnel

The Cross-Harbor Rail Freight Tunnel is envisioned as a two-mile tunnel under New York Harbor, from the Bay Ridge section of Brooklyn to Greenville Yards in Jersey City. This will link the existing Bay Ridge rail line (a below-grade, freight-only line through Brooklyn and Queens, owned by the Metropolitan Transportation Authority's Long Island Rail Road) with the nation's rail system in New Jersey.

The tunnel will allow much of our freight to move by rail into New York City, Long Island, Westchester, and southern Connecticut.

Three studies to advance the project have been completed to date: A 1995 New York City Preliminary Study, a 2000 Major Investment Study (conducted by the City of New York and the Federal Highway Administration), and the April 2004 Draft Environmental Impact Statement (EIS). These studies examined the costs and benefits of 60 alternative ways of moving goods into the region from west of the Hudson. The studies concluded that the "preferred alternatives" are either a one- or two-track rail freight tunnel under the Harbor.

The environmental impact study concluded that the Cross Harbor Tunnel has the highest benefit-to-cost ratio (2.2-to-1) of any major transportation project currently under consideration in New York. The estimated hard cost of constructing a two-track tunnel is $2.3 billion. Including soft costs—such as insurance and other administrative fees—and the costs of the required rail terminals, bridge clearance improvements and other necessary facilities, the total cost of a two-track tunnel project is estimated at $7.3 billion. The net present cost is $4 billion. A conservative estimate (even assuming zero induced economic development, which is difficult to quantify) of the net present value of the benefits is approximately $10.5 billion. This is a phenomenal return on investment, unheard of in other, similar endeavors.

Even a one-track tunnel, which may ultimately be advisable initially to save money, has an extremely high benefit-to-cost ratio of 1.9-to-1. A one-track tunnel and its associated infrastructure would cost about $1.8 billion. The second track could be added later, as the market and traffic volume dictate.

There are a number of other benefits that were confirmed by the environmental impact statement.

For one thing, the presence of the tunnel would mitigate congestion by generating a large shift of freight traffic from truck to rail in the region. A direct and efficient cross harbor link would also increase the competitiveness of freight rail in New York City and the region, competitiveness that is presently hindered because of outdated freight rail infrastructure and the lack of an efficient, high-capacity option for moving freight rail across the Hudson River. The environmental impact study also predicts that the Cross Harbor Tunnel would eliminate 2,800 daily truck trips, many going through some of the most congested choke points of the region. This is equivalent to a reduction of more than 10,000 daily car trips. Overall, the tunnel is projected to remove 1 million tractor trailers and 6 million vehicle miles traveled from New York City streets per year.

There are economic and employment considerations, too. The tunnel would act as a key engine for economic growth by creating as many as 30,000 new regional long-term jobs, with about 23,000 of them in the five boroughs of New York. In addition, it would create an additional 1,000 construction jobs.

Perhaps the most critical result of the tunnel would be that it would serve to improve New York's air quality and public health. The adverse effects of congestion from motor vehicle pollution take a huge and dramatic toll on the health of New Yorkers. There is a well-researched body of epidemiological studies from around the world that documents the serious threats associated with exposure to PM2.5, which are the sooty chemical particles produced by a number of sources, from car exhausts to power plans. They contribute to a number of health problems, including lower birth weight, asthma, cardiovascular and respiratory problems, strokes and heart attacks. Those conditions lead to increased use of asthma medication, doctor visits, emergency room trips, hospital admissions, school absenteeism and premature death. In 2000, New York City children were almost twice as likely to be hospitalized for asthma as children in the United States as a whole. Additionally, 94 percent of the added cancer risk from air pollutants in New York City comes from hazardous air pollutants released by vehicles. Our asthma rates in New York City and the region have risen as our freight rail network has deteriorated. The tunnel would remove 120,000 tons of carbon dioxide each year from our air.

Not insignificantly, the tunnel will provide important national security benefits by creating a key system redundancy that will ensure that essential goods can move into New York City and Long Island, even if a terrorist attack closed the George Washington or Verrazano-Narrows Bridges to trucks.

In 2008, when the Port Authority took over the project and resumed work on the environmental impact statement, it received $100 million in funds I obtained for the project in the 2005 federal transportation bill (called "SAFETEA-LU"). The Port Authority is working in earnest on the supplemental environmental impact statement, which will include updated land use and traffic data, new shipper surveys, analysis of mitigation and impacts, financial analysis, and selection of a preferred alternative.

Other recent events have been encouraging. Earlier this year, Governor David A. Paterson, a 20-year supporter of the tunnel concept, released the "New York State Rail Plan 2009: Strategies for a New Age," the first updated state rail plan in more than two decades. The plan specifically calls for implementation of the "identified recommendations of the Cross Harbor Freight Movement Project Environmental Impact Statement." This report obviously greatly enhances the ability of the Port Authority to move forward aggressively in its advocacy of the project.

Certainly there are those in the public debate who are inclined to argue that a crippling recession is hardly the ideal time to make such a huge investment. However, this is the time to firmly place our resources in a project that would relieve congestion, improve the quality of health and allow for more efficient freight transport in the area. With a president and a Congress that are more focused on sustainability issues than ever before, with city and state governments that have already begun work on decreasing automobile use and its impacts, and with thousands of advocates and citizens who have become educated on freight, transportation and public health problems, I think the tide is finally turning.

Jerrold Nadler is a member of the United States House of Representatives, representing New York's Eighth Congressional District, which includes Lower Manhattan, the borough's West Side and parts of Brooklyn.

GREEN BUILDINGS: A CRITICAL COMPONENT IN ECONOMIC RECOVERY

By Christine C. Quinn

Ever since the 22-story Flatiron Building was completed on a distinctive, triangular block in Manhattan in 1902, New York's skyline has been an iconic symbol of the city's identity. New York City has hundreds of skyscrapers and a total of about 1 million buildings, most of which were here long before anyone even thought about going green—or even knew what going green meant. But somehow, going green—the quest to protect the environment and reduce energy costs and emissions—must now become as much a symbol of the character of New York City's buildings as its skyscrapers and architectural distinction.

As our cityscape has changed over the last century so, too, have our priorities. We face new economic and environmental challenges that require new vision and leadership from local governments. We confront a wide range of challenges like rising fuel costs and declining air quality. These threats affect every facet of our lives, from our ability to create and maintain affordable housing to the dramatic need to improve public health. If we are going to keep New York a middle class city, we need to take steps today to ensure our long-term sustainability, both environmental and economical.

On Earth Day, Mayor Michael R. Bloomberg and I, along with a host of others, stood atop one of the city's green roofs and announced a first-of-its-kind legislative package that will upgrade the city's existing buildings with energy efficient technology and will, at the same time, create thousands of jobs in the process.

These bills will affect roughly 22,000 of the largest buildings in our city, making more than half of our square footage more energy efficient over the next two decades by utilizing existing, cost-effective technologies. Taken together, these measures will reduce the city's carbon footprint by 5 percent, a reduction on a scale equivalent to removing all of the carbon emissions of Oakland, California.

First, we are also going to require a benchmarking standard for city buildings. The fact is that 80 percent of our emissions come from buildings. And it's our belief that, by requiring buildings to monitor and measure their energy usage, we can set new standards by giving building owners the opportunity to clearly see just how efficient—or inefficient—their buildings may be.

We are also going to close a loophole in the adopted version of the International Energy Conservation Code. Right now, these standards must be adhered to only if more than 50 percent of a building is renovated. Because most renovations only deal with one particular space, there is no real incentive or requirement to install the latest efficient technologies. By closing the loophole, any time a renovation takes place in one of New York City's 1 million buildings, work would be required to conform to a set of easily applied standards, resulting in both a significant energy reduction and cost savings.

Another area where we can easily have a great impact on efficiency is in lighting. In New York City, lighting accounts for approximately 20 percent of the energy used in buildings and roughly 20 percent of a building's carbon emissions. There have been drastic improvements to lighting technology over the past few decades. Nonetheless, many buildings continue to use last century's technology. Making the switch to more modern lighting systems is an important and incremental step in reducing our overall carbon footprint.

However, benchmarking, renovations and better lighting will only carry us so far. We also need to find a way to make our existing infrastructure more efficient, and we can't depend on that to happen on its own. That's why we are going to require owners of existing buildings larger than 50,000 square feet to make cost-effective energy efficiency improvements to their buildings once every 10 years by conducting a top-to-bottom audit and retrofit of their buildings. Owners will only be required to make the improvements if they will pay for themselves in five years. Whether we're talking about the Empire State Building or the Chrysler Building, the icons of our skyline will become monuments to the greater and greener commitment of our city over the next decade.

These improvements will result in significant employment opportunities for our city as well. Making these buildings energy efficient is going to take a well-trained workforce. We're going to need auditors and contractors to meet the increased demand. And fortunately for us, New York City has always had a deep pool of talented and skilled labor professionals.

Working with our partners in labor and the construction industry, we are coming up with a plan to meet the needs of this burgeoning industry, an industry that could create as many as 19,000 jobs. And these are green jobs that will pay living wages—jobs that will stay right here in New York City.

Creating permanent green jobs is as important now to the sustainability of our city as it is to our financial health. As we continue to deal with the fallout from the city's financial collapse, what's becoming abundantly clear is there is a continued overreliance of our economy on the well-being of the financial markets. Across our city, we can see how the lack of credit on Wall Street is affecting the construction worker in, say, Astoria, Queens, by looking at the skeletons of unfinished buildings that are scattered throughout so many neighborhoods. Green jobs will create a line of employment that will be insulated from the ups and downs of the financial industry.

While increasing efficiency will ultimately lower utility bills and improve a building's financial fitness, there may be some buildings that can't immediately pay for the mandated efficiency improvements. To get this industry moving, we are going to establish a revolving loan fund by utilizing $16 million in federal funding from the American Recovery and Reinvestment Act. In the long run, especially if energy prices continue their upward trend, the private sector will no doubt embrace efficiency upgrades.

But in the meantime, a little nudge from government will go a long way toward getting this industry off the ground and getting money into the hands of the working families that need it the most.

The problems of the 21st Century, especially in these unsettling economic times, call for innovative solutions from local governments. These solutions must make our city more sustainable *and* stimulate our economy. And the Green Buildings Initiative will do just that. It's good for our environment; it will help save building owners about $750 million per year; and it will create thousands of jobs at a time when we desperately need them.

But even more importantly, a package like this ends the notion that going green somehow stands in the way of business owners making money. In fact, forward-looking polices like this ensure that—from the real estate magnate in Manhattan to the electrician in Staten Island who works to install new energy efficient lighting systems—prosperity will flow through every part of our city's economy.

Christine C. Quinn *is the speaker of the New York City Council.*

FIXING GOTHAM:
PUT PUBLIC INFRASTRUCTURE
AND TRANSPORTATION FIRST

By Nicole Gelinas

After years of unprecedented local and state boom in tax revenues—a period during which both the city and state reaped billions upon billions in unexpected tax windfalls year after year after year—New York still has, more or less, the same mass transportation system that it had before the boom started. And in the midst of the current recession, we are substantially behind many Asian and European nations in upgrading and expanding our mass transit system.

New York isn't simply waiting for an economic recovery. It's quite likely in the early stages of a wrenching economic readjustment. As Wall Street goes through its biggest structural change since the Great Depression, New York can no longer depend on a booming financial services industry to make up the core of its economy. There's no question that New York, provided it keeps up public safety, can attract new people, new industries and new jobs to replace the ones that are leaving. But it can only do so if it recognizes the worth of its most precious public-infrastructure asset (besides its water resources): its subway and bus system.

An aging, outdated infrastructure severely hampers the private sector's capacity to become more productive, harming our chances of a strong economic regeneration. Worse, though, it's possible—even probable—that New York is about to start an era of severe neglect of the aging assets that it *does* have. The state-run Metropolitan Transportation Authority faces a catastrophic decline in the local and state resources available to fund its next five-year capital budget, estimated to be more than $32 billion.

The problem will not be solved by the federal government, as seen in the paltry allocation to mass transit in the stimulus bill passed in February of 2009. Indeed, New York can expect just $1.3 billion for its transit investments from the stimulus.

Nor is the city likely to get the money from the private sector. While infrastructure projects built through "private-public partnerships" can be useful, if done right, for project and cost management, such projects still require significant public money. During the last boom, they depended on easy financing and banks' perceptions that the projects were risk-free. Today New York could not attract the private sector to new transit projects without offering significant government guarantees that would require the same fiscal resources as direct public financing.

But the solution is not for the MTA to pare back its capital budget, either. Consider: of $32 billion in projected capital spending over the next half decade, more than two thirds—$22 billion—is needed just to keep current assets in a state of acceptable repair. The MTA must spend $1 billion a year, for example, to replace obsolete signals. If it doesn't, and if it doesn't make similar investments in tracks and cars, the system will start to fall apart.

As for key expansion projects: now is not the time to cut back. The Second Avenue subway project, to alleviate dangerous overcrowding on the Upper East Side, for example, is decades overdue. It's true that the city and state should reprioritize their projects in a fiscal crisis. One could argue, persuasively, for example, that the $2.1 billion extension of the 7 train westward—to an undeveloped neighborhood—might not be the best use of limited resources in an economic recession.

But the savings should be directed toward other capital projects. The city and state should consider more ways for the MTA to expand the system through invisible but invaluable upgrades: retooling tracks and signals with 21st Century technology so that it wouldn't take more than an hour (with wait time) to travel from midtown Manhattan to many of the city's outer-borough neighborhoods.

Such spending constitutes investments in New York City itself. Consider the fact that the original construction of the subways encouraged mass residential development, often of working-class and middle-class neighborhoods. Re-investment in the transit system could encourage similar investment in aging neighborhoods. Faster commutes through modern technology would bring huge swaths of private, affordable housing much closer, time-wise, to the city's central business districts, improving residents' quality of life and encouraging developers to invest in working-class and middle-class neighborhoods far from Manhattan.

But where will the money come from?

In December 2008, a state commission headed by former MTA chair Richard Ravitch suggested that the state award the MTA new, permanent sources of tax revenues totaling $2.1 billion annually. The Ravitch panel suggested that the MTA raise $600 million annually from a new toll on the East River bridges, and $1.5 billion annually from a new payroll tax to be levied in the urban and regional counties that the authority serves.

The toll idea foundered. Imposing a sizable, new toll in this economic climate posed big risks to the economy and to the MTA. For one thing, in recent months, people have proven to be much more sensitive to increases in prices than they were just a few years ago. In November 2008, even after gas prices had declined, traffic on the MTA's bridges was down 5 percent from the previous year. In Indiana and Virginia, drivers have surprised highway officials by staying away from the roads in droves to avoid drastically higher tolls.

While political concerns eclipsed practical ones, there was no way of knowing how many people would choose to stay home on non-essential trips to avoid paying a new bridge toll. In early 2009, Fitch Ratings said of the MTA, that "loss of ridership and traffic due to city and regional job losses could have an impact on bridge and tunnel operating revenues greater than anticipated."

A higher-than-expected sensitivity to new tolls would have hurt Manhattan retailers, who are already struggling. It would have also hurt the MTA, which would have spent capital funds on the infrastructure to collect the tolls and have taken on a new financial burden of maintaining the bridges, currently done by the city, without getting the return expected.

Lawmakers enacted the other, even riskier, idea, to impose a new tax on payrolls in the MTA's service region. In terms of the economy, New Yorkers are already subject to the highest state and local income taxes in the nation—and more taxes are likely coming. Subjecting New Yorkers and residents of the larger region to another income-based tax, even if it is indirect, as this one is, would exacerbate this problem. It makes it more difficult for New York to attract the jobs it needs to replace Wall Street jobs.

Further, the fact that the payroll tax will fall on state, local, and county government payrolls (excepting public schools) in addition to private-sector payrolls means the private sector will pay twice, since the private sector funds government payrolls. And finally, the tax will fall on self-employed individuals. In New York City, self-employed entrepreneurs are already subject to a personal-tax burden beyond the regular income tax via the unincorporated business tax.

As for the MTA, the result will likely be extremely volatile since the new payroll tax is based on personal income. In the past six years, personal income growth in the MTA region has ranged from more than 10 percent annually to negative 3.6 percent. Such volatility will make it difficult to budget wisely from year to year, as recent volatility in the MTA's real-estate-related taxes has demonstrated.

Overall, the debate over which new taxes to implement for the MTA points to the real problem. Just as a hospital patient who has been repeatedly poked with needles often has no good veins left to tap, there are no good taxes left to increase in New York. To save and build upon its capital assets, New York must—finally—prioritize its existing spending, both within the MTA itself and in the larger state and city budgets.

Consider that one of the reasons for the MTA's current predicament is that its labor costs, largely pensions and health benefits for its labor force, have risen at a pace that far exceeds normal, predictable increases in revenues. Absent change, much of any new revenues will be quickly consumed by rising labor costs.

To put it in perspective, by 2012, the MTA's annual labor costs will have risen by nearly $700 million, consuming nearly one-third of the $2.1 billion in new funding sources that the state legislature enacted. Furthermore, the "draconian" service cuts that the pre-bailout MTA proposed last winter for New York City transit would have saved only $130 million annually in two years' time, while workers' benefits costs will have risen by the same amount.Any administrative or service cuts that the MTA can practically impose are easily Consumed by rising labor costs.

The state and city should decide whether the MTA's purpose is to provide vital mass-transit infrastructure to the private sector—or to provide its own workers with pension and health benefits that are no longer available in the private sector. The MTA can no longer do both—and it is not right to make the MTA's working-class constituents suffer via deterioration of their commutes in order to reward the few. Moreover, these issues do not just affect the MTA. Governor Paterson and Mayor Bloomberg have called for modest employee-benefits reforms in their own workforces.

In general, though, the MTA's perilous position is evidence that the rest of the state and city budgets are dangerously imbalanced. Consider: state-funded spending altogether is up more than 20 percent after inflation in the past five years. The state must start to make progress on issues like its Medicaid program, which spends more than any other state's program—more than $45 billion annually—without providing humane care to the elderly, among other things.

It would be far better for the state and for the MTA in the long term if New York would make progress in reforming its own budget. Then, the Legislature could take a greater portion of *existing* tax revenues and dedicate them formally and permanently to the MTA. The downstate sales tax and the gasoline tax are just two possibilities that could generate more dedicated, permanent revenue for the MTA, as well as, potentially, a small portion of the downstate income tax, capped to reduce volatility.

The MTA desperately needs more money—and the public needs for it to have more money. Otherwise, it risks deterioration in its most precious public physical assets. But the MTA can no longer be seen in isolation if the Legislature's fixes for it are to be anything but temporary.

The Legislature should make permanent room in the budget for mass transit. Indeed, another $1.5 to $1.8 billion for mass transit annually—out of a nearly $80 billion state-funds budget—is not asking much.

Nicole Gelinas, *a Chartered Financial Analyst, is a contributing editor to* City Journal *and a senior fellow at the Manhattan Institute.*

TIME FOR A NEW WPA? NEW YORK NEEDS INFRASTRUCTURE—AND JOBS

By Justin Davidson

O ver the past eight years—the time it has taken America to absorb the body blows of 9/11 and Katrina, launch two wars, watch its savings shrivel and its debt balloon, and elect its first black president—a team of experts has been studying the question of whether to fix the rickety old Tappan Zee Bridge or throw it out and buy a new one. The panel has finally plumped for the second option: a $16 billion juggernaut, with room for express buses and commuter rail. Hallelujah! Now all we have to do is rustle up the money, assume the budget will double, and wait another decade or two. That, and demand a design worthy of a Hudson crossing. The study group's report doesn't touch on that topic, as if actually designing a bridge were a finishing touch, something you do after the technical issues have been taken care of. Yet, the need for a new bridge is a chance to build a marvel. Which is why it's time to call an artist—say, Santiago Calatrava.

Calatrava is the world's preeminent magus of bridges, a wizard of white steel spans that are always performing some aerial flourish. Tapered masts point diagonally into the sky, tethered to a deck by fine white threads. Beams bend into parabolic curves and tilted arcs. Curving columns narrow as they meet the ground, recalling graceful ankles. His bridges deny their massive burdens and seem barely anchored to the earth. Calatrava is far from the only architect capable of building a Tappan Zee masterpiece, but his portfolio reminds us that we live in a time of wondrous spans.

In 1933, when Franklin Delano Roosevelt took office, much of the country was making do with Victorian bridges, horse-and-buggy roads, and improvised sanitation. FDR began binding the country together with sinews of concrete and cable. We need to do for the 21st Century what FDR did for the Twentieth—invest in worn-out highways, our frail electrical grid, our public transit, brittle bridges, and water supplies. A new New Deal, equipped with an Obama-era version of the Works Progress Administration, could put millions back to work, modernize the country, nudge the economy towards recovery, and produce a barrage of working monuments. It would be a stimulus package that keeps on stimulating long into the future.

This late-model WPA would take advantage of a moment when great architecture, buoyed by a long construction boom and debilitated by the bubble's pop, is looking for a purpose. The international corps of architectural auteurs, who have spent a decade or two dreaming up fantastical museums and ever more luxurious condos, could be challenged to build in American cities—particularly ours—on the grandest possible scale. They should be given the chance to tackle society's most massive, crucial, and abiding projects: viaducts, junctions, sewage plants, power plants, and bridges.

There are negative reasons to cultivate an interest in bridges—if you don't, they might fall down—but for positive reasons, consider the ring of noble behemoths with which the visionary engineer Othmar Ammann linked New York to the rest of the world. Clunkier structures would have done the job, but this would be a poorer city without the suite of elegant structures wrought by the Swiss-born engineer. In one amazing eight-year run, he opened the Bayonne, George Washington, Triborough, and Bronx Whitestone bridges, and followed up with the Throgs Neck and Verrazano-Narrows. Ammann considered himself as much responsible to the future as he was to his employers. For the George Washington Bridge, he drew up a gossamer colossus with steel latticework towers supporting a thin concrete deck. "Mere size and proportion are not the outstanding merit of a bridge," he said shortly after the dedication. "A bridge should be handed down to posterity as a truly monumental structure which will cast credit on the aesthetic sense of present generations."

Begun in plenty and completed in penury, the GWB heralded a decade of transformative public works, and we are still living off the Depression's handsome largesse. New Yorkers buy stamps at New

Deal post offices, snap a Frisbee across Central Park's New Deal lawns, dip below the Hudson through the New Deal's Lincoln Tunnel, and flush their toilets out to a New Deal sewage plant on Wards Island. The billions that FDR pumped into the physical environment are still reaping a return, a fact "that should be remembered in times when commitment to public life ebbs and belief rises that we simply cannot afford to invest," writes Robert D. Leighninger Jr. in his 2007 book *Long-Range Public Investment: The Forgotten Legacy of the New Deal.* "There was a time in our history when people found ways to combat despair by building for the future. The evidence is all around us." Next time you meet someone old enough to have paid taxes during the thirties, say, "Thank you."

We gawp at previous generations' epic feats of engineering yet relegate their modern equivalents to the eye-glazing category of *Infrastructure.* That bleak word applies mostly to places people rush through or avoid entirely. Nobody wants to linger in even the nicest airport or have an elegant incinerator next door. Everyone is in favor of sending waste away, but do we really have to think about it, or put that new water-treatment plant... here?

The result of this thoughtlessness is a nation of decrepitude. Barry LePatner, a construction lawyer who wrote the book *Broken Buildings, Busted Budgets,* is a Cassandra of infrastructure, bristling with alarming statistics. According to the United States Department of Transportation, 38 percent of New York State's 17,361 bridges are either "structurally deficient" or "functionally obsolete." The numbers are similar in New Jersey and Connecticut. "If you knew that your children on the school bus were crossing a structurally deficient bridge, no different from the I-35W in Minneapolis"—which collapsed in August 2007, killing 13 people—"would you stand quietly by?" LePatner says. "Until Americans understand that, we're not going to attend to this problem and we'll see an increasing number of bridges collapse." Elected officials know they stand to gain more from opposing one of these projects than from nudging it along. "Anyone in office who is told 'We need $80 million to repair this bridge' is going to say, 'If I have $80 million coming to my state, I'd rather use it for a park and have a ribbon-cutting,'" says LePatner.

During the presidential campaign, Barack Obama floated a proposal for a National Infrastructure Reinvestment Bank, which would deploy $60 billion over ten years to guarantee loans and assist localities in floating bond issues. That sounds like a lot of money until you start going through the country's to-do list. The American Society of Civil Engineers concluded in a 2005 study that the country's infrastructure was rotting faster than it could be repaired and that it would cost $1.6 trillion to avert a plague of exhausted levees, rampant blackouts, crumbling bridges, dysfunctional trains, and streams of filth gushing into waterways.

A new Tappan Zee has been—and will be—a hard sell, and a Calatrava design would enliven those who are just waiting to cry boondoggle. The public generally gives the thumbs-down to projects with awesome costs, geological timetables, and abundant opportunities for mismanagement, corruption, inconvenience, and environmental misery. Naysayers will point out that Calatrava's latest achievement, a footbridge in Venice, wound up costing four times its original budget. The blame for overruns, however, usually lies more in muddled management than in elegant design. Since the price of a new bridge climbs constantly, it's the delays and fumbles that make the price balloon. Good design can save money, trimming construction time and demanding more work from stronger steel. Ammann, for example, brought in the George Washington Bridge $5 million under budget.

In recent years, bridges have acquired fresh flights of possibility. Thanks to technological advances, a new bridge can weigh less, stretch farther, endure longer, and bear more traffic than ever. The great span of Norman Foster's 2004 highway viaduct in Millau, France, resembles a consort of stringed instruments, lifted on slender concrete-and-steel pillars high above the valley floor. A vertical gash appears in each pylon as it rises to the roadway, so that from certain angles it appears that the traffic passes through the eye of a needle. Or consider the Millennium Bridge in Gateshead, England, designed by Wilkinson Eyre, a lovely, lyrelike thing. Its pair of steel bows strung with filaments swivels up to let ships pass beneath the arcs or down to offer pedestrians a curving boardwalk.

New York, after decades of neglecting its engineering monuments, has lately taken better care of basic maintenance than most cities do, and it's fitfully capable of thinking big. The cataclysm at ground zero unstoppered a geyser of entrepreneurial thinking that has produced some fine if fantastical ideas. The architect Eytan Kaufman, to take one if-only instance, has worked out an alluring vision for a mile-long Rialto linking the Javits Center with Weehawken, New Jersey. The Hudson World Bridge would be a car-free playland of lawns and plazas, with a blimp-shaped convention or exhibit hall suspended overhead. It'll never happen, but without such untethered imagination, nothing else would, either.

One of the best places to seek uplift about the city's infrastructure is atop a cluster of stainless-steel-clad silos churning 200 million pounds of human waste. At Polshek Partnership's Newtown Creek Wastewater Treatment Plant, two quartets of shiny new "digester eggs" on blue-glazed pedestals rise over Greenpoint's industrial flatlands, dazzling motorists on the Long Island Expressway. A glassed-in catwalk links their peaks, affording views of midtown Manhattan and the seamless bulk of the great machines.

From that perch, you can see the future and smell the past. In six years or so, a closed system will trap the plumes from the plant's remaining 40-year-old open tanks, so schoolchildren won't wrinkle their noses when they file into the visitor center. Yes, visitor center: There, a fountain designed by Vito Acconci dodges between indoors and out, reminding the neighborhood that this epic-scaled apparatus is meant to cleanse water and return it to nature. At night, the eggs are washed in blue light, courtesy of the lighting genius Hervé Descottes, who turned the plant into an urban beacon visible from Manhattan's East Side high-rises. Prada recently scouted the complex for a photo shoot. "You can't hide it, so flaunt it," says Jim Pynn, the plant's enthusiastic superintendent, with a grin. That would make a fine motto for infrastructure's next wave.

Justin Davidson is a classical music and architecture critic with New York magazine. A version of this essay originally appeared in New York magazine.

STRENGTHENING VULNERABLE COMMUNITIES

BUILDING AN URBAN FOOD SYSTEM FOR THE 21ST CENTURY

By Nevin Cohen

The American Recovery and Reinvestment Act—a.k.a. the stimulus bill—gave Supplemental Nutrition Assistance Program (SNAP) recipients a 13.6 percent increase in their monthly food stamp benefits, enhancing this small but critical cushion against hunger during the current recession. For the 1.3 million New Yorkers who rely on SNAP benefits to make ends meet, the increase means an additional average $18 per month per person on top of the current average monthly benefits of $135, easing the burden of putting food on the table while paying for rent and other necessities.

Increasing SNAP food payments is a time-tested strategy for priming the economy during downturns because recipients spend the dollars immediately. Unlike stimulus projects that involve infrastructure, no blueprints need to be drawn up or construction permits obtained before money flows into the economy. And the multiplier effects are substantial. The United States Department of Agriculture estimates that every additional dollar in food benefits generates $1.84 in economic activity—and that every $5 billion in new SNAP dollars will create some 82,000 jobs. (For those who don't recognize SNAP, that's the new name for food stamps, which took effect in October 2008 as part of the updated Farm Bill.)

There is no question that low-income residents need more resources to feed their families, but those dollars should flow into a redesigned food system. With the right local policies that enable SNAP recipients to spend their benefits on healthier, locally produced fare, these food dollars can become another "stimulus" toward building an urban food system for the 21st century. Across New York City, we have too many neighborhoods where nourishing food is simply unavailable—at the same time that we have many enthusiastic food pioneers who want to plant (not pave) our route to a fresher future.

Now's the time to redouble our efforts to increase access to fresh fruits and vegetables, which will not only improve the nutritional status of low-income families who suffer disproportionately from diet-related diseases like obesity, diabetes and heart disease—but will support local farmers throughout the region, help to sustain agricultural communities, and protect ecologically sensitive areas (like New York City's own Catskill watershed) from harmful development.

In the short run, these policies should include steps to make locally grown fruits and vegetables more accessible to SNAP recipients and others living in low-income neighborhoods. Many neighborhoods in New York City lack even the most rudimentary food stores. In a recent survey of supermarket density in New York, the New York City Department of City Planning found that an estimated 3 million residents—more than one third of New Yorkers—live in neighborhoods with insufficient supermarkets or groceries that sell fresh fruits and vegetables.

Farmers markets can help to fill this gap during the growing season, and their popularity in even the poorest neighborhoods demonstrates strong unmet demand for fresh produce in a wide range of communities. By enabling producers to sell directly to consumers with no middlemen, these markets often sell produce and fruits that are fresher and less expensive than food sold in supermarkets and bodegas.

More SNAP recipients would shop at farmers markets if they could spend their food dollars, disbursed through electronic benefit cards, in more of the existing markets. In about one third of the city's farmers markets, support from city and state officials, particularly the Department of Agriculture and Markets and the Council on the Environment of NYC, has enabled the purchase of handheld wireless electronic benefit transfer (EBT) readers so the markets can accept food stamps. Funding an expansion of the farmers market EBT program to buy more card readers and provide wireless access, along with bookkeeping staff to process payments, would help more SNAP recipients stretch their benefits and incorporate more fresh fruits and vegetables into their diets. And every additional federal dollar captured at a farmers market supports local farmers instead of growers thousands of miles away.

In addition to farmers markets, mobile carts are an inexpensive and flexible model for retailing fruits and vegetables in low-income neighborhoods. The New York City Department of Health and Mental Hygiene estimates that only 10 percent of New York's mobile vendors sell fresh fruits and vegetables, but under a new program being rolled out by that department this year, the city will issue up to 1,000 new vendor licenses to "green carts" that sell only fresh fruits and vegetables in the neighborhoods with the lowest reported produce consumption. The green carts will not only make buying produce convenient in neighborhoods underserved by storefront green grocers or supermarkets, but they will help support a network of a thousand entrepreneurial retailers.

Bodegas are ubiquitous throughout the five boroughs, but they typically sell unhealthy beverages and processed food. The city has reached out to 400 bodegas to help them identify, stock, and promote the sale of fruits and vegetables that are in demand in their neighborhoods. For a pilot sample of bodegas, the Department of Health has even provided free local produce to demonstrate the viability of marketing fruits and vegetables. Some bodegas are receiving help in carrying produce from local farmers markets. Expanding this marketing assistance, as well as providing financing for the refrigeration infrastructure needed to stock fresh produce, is critical to ensure that bodegas are able to profit from selling healthier foods, potentially transforming them into full-fledged green grocers.

Encouraging the development of medium-sized grocery stores and supermarkets in neighborhoods with low-income residents would increase access to fresh foods and reduce costs to consumers. Proposed policies (the Food Retail Expansion to Support Health, or FRESH program) that support supermarket development include density bonuses, to allow developers in targeted neighborhoods to build larger supermarkets than permitted by existing zoning, and districts zoned for light manufacturing allowing supermarkets as of right. Supermarkets could be exempted from property or business taxes or could be allowed abatements under commercial abatement programs. Public agencies could also be directed to design space for food retailers in city apartment buildings, office buildings, and other projects. These efforts to advance supermarket-friendly land use and economic policies are being advanced by the Mayor and City Council Speaker, with the support of the Manhattan Borough President, food advocates, and labor unions.

But one critical bricks-and-mortar project would make a huge improvement to our food system. Transforming the recently-opened wholesale Greenmarket into a larger, permanent wholesale farmers market would make it dramatically more profitable for midsize farmers to sell their fresh products in New York. By one estimate, such a market would enable some 250 farmers to distribute their products in the city, making it economically viable for grocery stores, schools, hospitals and restaurants to buy a reliable supply of local food. The economic benefits of this project are significant. Market studies predict that a New York City wholesale farmers market would sell $85 million worth of local farm products, generating $142 million a year in total economic activity and 1,650 new jobs. The project was a priority for former Governor Spitzer, and the Paterson administration should similarly commit future recovery dollars to this essential facility.

Much of the current federal stimulus package has been directed towards rebuilding highways and federal buildings. But investing in our neglected urban food system is critical for cities like New York facing hunger and food insecurity, high rates of diet-related diseases, and a struggling regional agriculture sector. Policies to direct federal food dollars to local food producers, distributors and retailers, and new infrastructure, such as a wholesale farmers market, will make it economical for small and medium-size farms to compete in the global food market. Together with the robust network of grassroots organizations working to create community gardens and urban farms, community supported agriculture programs, and educational programs to rebuild culinary skills, these steps will result in sustainable urban food systems that make our cities fairer, more environmentally sound, and healthier.

Nevin Cohen *is assistant professor of environmental studies at The New School. A version of this essay originally appeared in* City Limits *magazine.*

THE NEED TO RESTRUCTURE NEW YORK CITY'S PERSONAL INCOME TAX

By Amy M. Traub

New York City's tax code offers a meaningful opportunity for ensuring that the pain of a poor economy is shared fairly. Tax reforms can also stimulate the city's economy by putting more money into the hands of low- and moderate-income New Yorkers who will spend it quickly. And when the city ultimately emerges from recession, a rebalanced personal income tax can remain a force for equity in the most unequal city in the nation.

Undoubtedly, the current economic downturn is being felt by all New Yorkers in one way or another. But some are better equipped to weather the slump than others. In the boom years, Wall Street profits soared, real estate values skyrocketed, and the city's population of multimillionaires increased. Yet even in 2006, with the economy in full swing, nearly a fifth of New York's population—1.5 million people—lived below the federal poverty threshold. Nearly half of the city's poor families were headed by a working person who earned wages too low to lift his or her family out of poverty. Just above these working poor households, an additional 19 percent of city residents lived on the borderline of poverty, striving to earn a middle-class standard of living for their families. For many New Yorkers, the squeeze was on long before the recession hit.

Recognizing the difficulty low- and moderate-income working families face making ends meet in our high-cost city, New York has taken a number of steps in recent years to reduce taxes on these households. For example, New York introduced its own earned income tax credit in 2002 and added a child care tax credit in 2007. But despite these efforts, the city's tax base still relies on revenue from households with such modest incomes that the federal and state governments have exempted them from taxation entirely. Currently 224,200 low-and moderate-income New York City households are obligated to pay New York City income taxes even though they owe no federal and/or state income taxes. The Drum Major Institute for Public Policy proposes eliminating New York City personal income taxes on these aspiring middle-class households.

We pay for this tax cut with a small marginal tax increase on New Yorkers with a taxable income of more than $500,000 a year—the 1.4 percent of city households who benefited most from New York's economic boom. The tax increase would affect a projected 43,400 households. These changes to the New York City tax code would require approval of the New York City and New York State governments.

The DMI plan would eliminate city taxes for approximately 717,700 New Yorkers, including 281,000 adults and 436,700 dependent children. The proposal applies only to households that both owe no federal and/or state income taxes and have a taxable annual income of less than $40,000. Roughly two-thirds of the beneficiaries have taxable incomes of less than $20,000. Virtually all the beneficiaries are households with children—in fact, nearly one in four New York children lives in a household that would receive a tax cut. Single parents, struggling to raise a family on their own would be the largest group to benefit. On average, affected households would get a $321 tax cut as a result of eliminating their city income taxes. Households with a taxable income between $20,000 and $30,000 would see $533 in annual city taxes eliminated.

New York City currently brings in approximately $71.9 million in annual revenue from its personal income tax on low- and moderate-income households who owe no state and/or federal taxes. To replace this revenue, and provide a cushion should revenue projections fall short, DMI advocates raising an additional $100 million. This is a tiny amount in the scope the city's budget. It amounts to approximately 1.3 percent of projected revenue from the city's personal income tax in 2008 and just under two-tenths of one percent (0.17 percent) of total projected city revenue in 2008.

To generate the necessary tax revenue, DMI proposes a new tax bracket on annual incomes higher than $500,000. Wealthy households in the new bracket would pay taxes at a base rate of 3.285 percent—a 0.085 percentage point increase from the current top base tax rate of 3.2 percent. This amounts to a tax increase of less than one tenth of one percentage point on these households. For example, households making $550,000 a year would owe about $48 more in taxes under the proposal, while those with an income of $600,000 annually would owe the city just $97 more per year.

Critics argue that the poor economy, coupled with the city's budget squeeze, makes this a bad time to offer a tax cut. In fact, this tax reform is particularly timely in today's grim economic climate. It will provide direct tax savings to working families with modest incomes that may otherwise have little to cushion them during the downturn. But the benefits will spread beyond the households that are direct beneficiaries: by putting more money into the hands of squeezed, low- and moderate-income families likely to spend it immediately, New York can stimulate the economy in its neighborhoods and city-wide. Meanwhile, studies suggest that the wealthy households called to pay increased taxes are unlikely to reduce their consumption much, if at all, as a result.

What's more, because the tax increase on households making more than $500,000 is very small, it is highly unlikely that any household would consider relocating outside the city to avoid it. The end result provides both economic stimulus and assistance to vulnerable New York City households, paid for by those New Yorkers who benefited most from the city's expansion.

Yet DMI's income tax reform is more than a short-term response to hard times. It is an enduring statement of principles: New York's tax code should rely most heavily on those households that have profited most from the city's substantial public investments in such areas as efficient transportation, an educated workforce, low crime, clean streets, and livable neighborhoods. New York is the most unequal state in the nation and income disparities are even more extreme in New York City. Over the last 30 years, income inequality in the city has grown rapidly, with the wealthiest 20 percent of New York City families seeing their incomes grow nearly six times faster than the bottom 80 percent.

Income is even more concentrated among the top 1 percent and 2 percent of New York City's households. This evidence suggests that the wealthiest New Yorkers benefited disproportionately from the last two economic expansions. As New York now faces far more difficult economic times, these households should now be asked to make a greater contribution to their city and to their struggling neighbors. At the same time, the city should not put an additional barrier in the path of families struggling to make ends meet and to work their way into the middle class. And finally, the city can boost these aspiring middle-class families without shifting taxes onto those New Yorkers who have already managed to attain a middle-class standard of living.

In 2007, DMI surveyed 101 prominent New Yorkers from all sectors of the city, asking their views of the state of the city's middle class and seeking policies that would help to strengthen and expand it. The overwhelming majority of respondents favored making New York City's personal income taxes more progressive. This modest realignment of the tax code is a first step toward a more substantial revision. For that reason, and because the reform is meant to be permanent, we propose a new tax bracket—rather than a temporary surcharge—at the $500,000 level. While the increased tax rate at this level is trivial, it signals the direction the city must go to make its tax code fairer.

As another signpost for further reform, DMI proposes automatically adjusting the $40,000 cutoff point for eliminating city personal income taxes for inflation. Indexing taxes to inflation ensures that city taxes do not shift back onto low- and moderate-income households over time. Currently, most of New York's city and state taxes are not indexed to inflation: as a result, they become less progressive over time as more and more households fall into the higher brackets. The federal tax code, in contrast, is indexed to inflation—with the exception of Alternative Minimum Tax, which Congress hurriedly adjusts every year to avoid raising taxes on middle-class households. To preserve the progressive elements of New York's tax code, the entire personal income tax system should ultimately be indexed to inflation.

Of course, DMI's proposed restructuring of the New York City personal income tax alone will not solve the city's fiscal crisis. But this rebalancing of the city's personal income tax structure is an ideal complement to the necessary revenue increases: it would provide an extra boost to the low- and middle-income New Yorkers who are among the hardest hit by the ailing economy, while also stimulating the city's overall economy by putting money into the hands of those likely to spend it. Finally, it would establish principles that should guide the city's efforts to raise revenue. And the wealthiest New Yorkers, who have benefited disproportionately from the city's economic boom, should be asked to contribute most now that leaner times have come.

Amy M. Traub is the research director at the Drum Major Institute for Public Policy.

IN PLANNING FOR ANY ECONOMIC REBOUND, RACE MATTERS

By Jacob Faber

The country and the New York region are in crisis. Wall Street is the epicenter of the financial earthquake that has rocked our city, nation, and world. Home foreclosure rates are skyrocketing while families struggle to meet a rising cost of living in the face of lost or reduced earnings. Pensions are threatened, and college is becoming less affordable. States and cities face fiscal crises. These are hard realities, but we can make things better.

Not surprisingly, race all too often determines opportunity. Second-ring suburbs are high-opportunity areas and remain overwhelmingly white, while the large majority of people of color live in urban areas, or in older, declining, inner-ring suburbs, where jobs are scarce, housing is of poor quality, and schools are failing. These low-opportunity areas also have smaller tax bases and struggle to build infrastructure or provide needed services.[1]

As the city seeks now to emerge from the recession, we must look to communities of color and low opportunity areas to understand what we can do differently to produce stronger and more equitable opportunity structures, such as healthy credit markets. We must also ensure that well-intentioned policies do not harm or fail to help communities of color. Sharing the burdens and benefits of public policy is not only fair but can ensure a strong economy and a healthy environment.

The choices we make now can either create jobs and build long-term opportunity for everyone or widen the gap between rich and poor and cause us to falter yet again in the future. To make the right decisions, we need to look at the entire region and identify communities with limited opportunities. This will tell us where to make investments. It takes a regional perspective to understand how suburban sprawl and decentralized growth have made all communities more vulnerable. And while municipal and tax boundaries may separate jurisdictions on a map, the fates of cities and suburbs are connected.[2]

The current crisis has its roots in housing discrimination. The burst of the housing bubble has many complex and interrelated causes, but one factor is predatory lending and its prevalence in the under-regulated subprime market, both of which have their roots in mortgage discrimination. Policy decisions made over the years have helped make communities of color much more vulnerable to unfair practices. New Deal and post-World War II policies created the middle class by making homeownership much more affordable. Yet those policies also discriminated against people of color. For example, 99 percent of the 67,000 GI Bill mortgages in New York and the suburbs of northern New Jersey went to white veterans.[3] Federal subsidies for highways and infrastructure further fueled racialized suburbanization as not only people, but jobs, fled cities.[4]

These bad policies made communities of color the most financially vulnerable and credit-starved and helped create a market for the subprime mortgage industry; therefore, it should be no surprise that subprime loans and foreclosures have hit communities of color particularly hard.

Here are some significant facts: Nationally, more than 2 million Americans are projected to lose their homes in the coming year and over 40 million neighboring homes will suffer declines in value (a total of $352 billion in lost home equity nationally).[5] Up to $200 billion of this lost equity previously belonged to people of color.[6] Significantly, black and Latino homeowners are much more likely to have sub-prime mortgages than their white counterparts even when they have the same income.[7] And in New York City, black borrowers were 12 times more likely and Latino borrowers almost eight times more likely than white residents to receive a higher-cost, home-purchase loan.[8]

In fact, the region is growing and becoming more diverse, but racialized isolation persists. New York City and the surrounding region are growing largely because of immigration. Since 2000, Asian and Latino population growth accelerated, while the size of black and white populations changed little.[9] However, people of color and immigrants largely remain isolated from opportunity. Limited transportation options, diminishing affordable housing and other challenges make it difficult for people of color to commute to or move near job centers.

Another critical issue is the fact that opportunity is not equally distributed throughout the region. To understand the relationship between housing, education, jobs, and health, the Center for Social Inclusion developed an Opportunity Index, which measures wellbeing on the neighborhood level.[10]

Low-opportunity areas do not have access to good housing, well-paying jobs, a healthy environment or good schools. High-opportunity areas, compared to others in the region, do have good housing, access to career ladders, and schools that prepare children to participate in the economy.

The Opportunity Index makes visible the dramatic differences in opportunity across the region. Most high-opportunity areas are in second-ring suburbs in Northern New Jersey, Long Island, Downstate New York, and Connecticut. Urban areas in the region, with a few exceptions (Lower Manhattan and parts of Brooklyn, for example), are characterized by low opportunity, as are some rural areas north and west of New York City and parts of Long Island.

The Opportunity Index shows a clear trend: White Americans are more likely to have greater access to opportunity, while people of color are largely trapped in low-opportunity areas. Black, Latinos, and Asian Americans made up 44 percent of the region's population in 2006, but 88 percent of the region's very low opportunity areas. White residents, who represent 54 percent of the region's population, account for 88 percent of very high opportunity areas.

There are many reasons opportunity is low in communities of color. The region is diversifying, but racialized isolation is still a huge issue.

Economic opportunity—especially for the poor—is dwindling as we move more towards a two-tiered, service-sector economy. Affordable housing is disappearing; and the areas where it still stands often lack good jobs, schools, and other important services. The education system continues to perpetuate inequality, which hurts the region's wellbeing by creating an unskilled workforce. Patterns of growth and development—intentional and unintentional—have resulted in the concentration of environmental burdens and created unhealthy, unsustainable communities. All of these trends are connected and mutually reinforcing. As long as we continue to leave people out of growth and prosperity, the vitality of the region is at risk.

There are several policy recommendations that would help to create an equitable and inclusive region. The New York region needs policies and investments that target those in greatest need to promote a thriving economy and more socially cohesive region. Policies have created both avenues and barriers to good housing, jobs, education, transportation, and health, and a clean, safe environment. Inequitable growth has not only starved communities of color of opportunity, it has weakened the region's resilience as a whole.

For one thing, there is a need to create incentives for opportunity-based housing.

Where housing is located matters just as much as whether it is affordable. Housing authorities in the region should work together to support the location of Low Income Housing Tax Credit units in high-opportunity areas. By giving low-income people of color choices about where to live, we create opportunities for them to increase their access to decent jobs and schools. The criteria should reflect the range of factors that influence access to opportunity: proximity to job centers and critical amenities, school quality, socioeconomic diversity, and others.[11]

Governments should make inclusionary zoning mandatory for housing development, requiring builders to include a certain amount of housing units affordable for low- and moderate-income households within market-rate housing developments. In exchange, builders get to build more units than the number allowed by the zoning ordinance. This policy can insure greater socioeconomic diversity. To create housing that is truly affordable for low- and moderate-income residents, affordability must be defined in relation to the local context of real median wages and the local housing market.[12] Housing must also remain permanently affordable and keep pace with changing market conditions

Secondly, it is critical to make communities of color partners in the regional economy. Investing in communities of color as regional business partners is key to spurring the innovation necessary to diversify the economy and compete globally. To take advantage of growing market opportunities, the region should develop entrepreneurship and labor in low-opportunity communities. The region should also invest in connecting those in low-opportunity areas to high-opportunity areas by expanding quality transit.

Local and state governments must create incentive programs to help small, locally owned businesses in low opportunity communities get the capital investment and support they need. Several first steps could include creating a small-business assistance fund, securing affordable commercial space specifically for small businesses. Other important goals would be ensuring community and small business participation in development decisions. Another goal would be implementing long-term protections for small businesses, such as rent control, limits on big box store construction, and the end of eminent domain for private development.[13]

Economic stimulus investments from the federal government are likely to go mostly to construction and repair projects.[14] Because people of color are under-represented in construction jobs, "shovel ready" projects funded by a stimulus package will not benefit many unemployed people of color without specific incentives and enforcement tools. The stimulus package should require local resident hiring and apprenticeships.

An additional policy recommendation would be to develop fiscal policies that build regional opportunity for those in greatest need. The region needs to create new fiscal policies that distribute public revenues in ways that build regional prosperity. Fiscal policies that focus on strengthening the region benefit all municipalities because they reduce competition within the region and increase its capacity to attract and retain quality business growth and development.[15] Done right, revenue sharing can attract good development and good jobs, reduce long-term fiscal costs, and improve intergovernmental cooperation.[16]

Also, it is essential to establish land use policies to protect and empower residents. Land use planning processes must facilitate meaningful community participation. This means that development must be connected to the regional economy and prioritize community needs and vision. Planning should ensure that locally owned businesses and low-income residents will benefit from zoning changes and development plans. Municipalities should also consider the long-term impacts zoning decisions will have on building or eroding opportunities in a neighborhood.

Additionally, it is critical that we invest to an even greater degree in education. One step that states and cities can take to improve educational quality is greater investment in school construction to reduce class size. Municipalities should target school construction in communities with rapidly growing populations and overcrowded schools. In addition to shrinking class sizes, these investments would also provide much needed jobs in teaching and construction.

School districts in the region can also take budget-neutral steps that would substantially improve educational outcomes across race. For example, policies to eliminate academic tracking in middle schools and high schools have been extremely successful in increasing educational opportunity for all students.[17]

Another policy imperative would be to preserve and support the existing healthcare infrastructure in underserved communities. Cities and states must be poised to use federal resources for equitable healthcare infrastructure everyone can access. One step is to halt closures and downsizings of hospitals in underserved communities. Further, government should develop new facilities and modernize health information technology in areas where health opportunity and primary care is particularly low.[18] Investing in primary care infrastructure and community health centers would both reduce health disparities and trim long-term healthcare costs by hundreds of millions of dollars.[19]

State and local governments should create a pipeline of medical professionals from the most medically underserved communities. Investing in the ability of communities of color to participate in the growing healthcare profession provides a double benefit. Not only are professionals from medically underserved communities more likely to work in communities that most need their services but providing good jobs with career ladders also invests in their economic mobility.

And lastly, we must increase fresh food options in underserved communities. Zoning and land use regulations linked to community planning establishments can create incentives that encourage the placement of supermarkets and cooperatives in underserved communities.[20] Locally owned and operated businesses benefit local communities more directly because the average dollar spent at these establishments tends to recycle more times in the local economy.[21] Cities and states should also use zoning, land use regulations, and public incentives to encourage the development of small businesses and community-owned cooperatives that provide fresh food.[22]

These steps would go a long way toward helping the city emerge from its current economic difficulties and produce stronger and more equitable opportunity structures for all New Yorkers.

Jacob Faber is a senior researcher at The Center for Social Inclusion.

Endnotes

1   Robert D. Bullard, ed., *The Black Metropolis in the Twenty-First Century: Race, Power, and Politics of Place* (Maryland: Rowman and Littlefield Publishers, Inc, 2007), 97.

2   Manuel Pastor et al., *Regions That Work: How Cities and Suburbs Can Grow Together* (University of Minnesota Press, 2000), 3.

3   Meizhu, Lui, et. al. *The Color of Wealth: The Story Behind the U.S. Racial Wealth Divide* (New York: The New Press, 2006), 257.

4   Jonathan Bowles and Qianqi Shen, "New York by the Numbers: Economic snapshots of the five boroughs," *Center for an Urban Future*, vol. 1 (October 2008).

5   "Updated Projections of Subprime Foreclosures in the United States and Their Impact on Home Values and Communities" Center for Responsible Lending, September 23, 2008.

6   Amaad Rivera, et. al., "Foreclosed: State of the Dream 2008," *United for a Fair Economy*, 2008.

7   Allen J. Fishbein, Patrick Woodall, "Subprime Locations: Patterns of Geographic Disparity in Subprime Lending", Consumer Federation of America, September 5, 2006.

8   Jim Campen et al., "Paying More for the American Dream: A Multi-State Analysis of Higher Cost Home Purchase Lending," *California Reinvestment Coalition,* March 2007, ii.

9   U.S. Census Decennial Census 2000 Summary File 3 and U.S. Census 2006 American Community Survey.

10 A complete methodology is available in our 2009 report "One Region: Promoting Prosperity Across Race."

11 John A. Powell et al., Communities of Opportunity: A Framework for a More Equitable and Sustainable Future for All (2007).

12 Nicholas Brunick, Lauren Goldberg, and Susannah Levine, Business and Professional People for the Public Interest, *Voluntary of Mandatory Inclusionary Housing? Production, Predictability, and Enforcement* (2004).

13 *Families United for Racial and Economic Equality and the Urban Justice Center* "Out of Business: The Crisis of Small Business in Rezoned Downtown Brooklyn," July 2008.

14 MacGillis, Alec and Michael D. Shear "Stimulus Package To First Pay for Routine Repairs" Washington Post December 14, 2008.

15 Myron Orfield, Thomas Luce & Amerigis LLC, Northeast Ohio Economic Revenue Study (February 2008).

16 Orfield, Luce and Ameregis.

17 Angela Glover Blackwell et al., Regionalism: Growing Together to Expand Opportunity for All (May 2007).

18 Rosenbaum, Sara, et. al. "Laying the Foundation Health System Reform in New York State and the Primary Care Imperative," June 2006, 31.

19 The Opportunity Agenda, "Dangerous & Unlawful: Why Our Health Care System Is Failing New York And How to Fix It" 2006, 58–59.

20 "Going to Market: New York City's Neighborhood Grocery Store and Supermarket Shortage" New York City Department of City Planning. October 2008.

21 PolicyLink website "Healthy Food Retailing: Why Use It?" (accessed January 13, 2009).

22 Angotti, Tom. "Can Planners Help New Yorkers Eat Better?" *Gotham Gazette*, June 2008.

THE SCENE IS BETTER FOR IT:
ARTISTIC AND CULTURAL LIVELIHOODS

Dan Morris

The nation's biggest public source of arts and culture funding is not the National Endowment for the Arts, as many might believe. It's actually New York City's Department of Cultural Affairs (DCA), boasting an annual expense budget of around $150 million and a $1 billion capital budget for the next five years.[1] The agency finances artistic and cultural endeavors that generate jobs, wages and tax revenue. Massive institutions like the Metropolitan Museum of Art tend to receive the most sizeable grants because, on the surface at least, their economic impact is correspondingly large. City Hall reads very literally analysis from the Alliance for the Arts revealing that "the operating budgets of several large organizations account for a major part of total expenditures by nonprofit arts organizations in New York City."[2]

Too literally, it turns out. Focusing on what happens at the top makes it easy to miss the action down below. More investment in improving how artists and cultural producers live and work—paying attention to individuals and communities, not just institutions—would yield greater returns, especially among underground influencers who start trends and build brands that profitably penetrate the mainstream. They hold far more growth and revenue potential than aging museums that simply put tradition on display and could survive on private philanthropy and still appeal to wealthy residents and tourists, which, let's be honest, is their goal. To support new talent and human capital in the creative sector, DCA must nurture unconventional careers, fostering diverse scenes and inclusive milieus capable of sustaining them.

That won't happen if the agency continues to dole out money mainly to assist leaders of prominent organizations rather than ordinary people who are struggling freelancers. Its grant-making is caught between largesse for insiders and laissez-faire for outsiders. Those who can withstand expert scrutiny and exploit credentials and connections to compete for funds are rewarded; others whose lesser reputations or eccentric ideas don't easily fit onto grant applications are left alone to succeed or fail. Neither approach benefits the many thousands of independent, unaffiliated people trying to earn a decent and interesting living based on what they create and how others enjoy their creations.

DCA staff should look beyond data on organizational expenditures and get reacquainted with *The Culture Consumers*, Alvin Toffler's strikingly relevant book from the 1960s, where he explains the inefficiency of art.[3] "It's not that the production of art is becoming any less efficient than it ever was," he writes, "but that its level of efficiency is falling farther and farther behind that of the economy as a whole. Indeed, in this very difference lies much of the attractiveness and appeal of art... The farther we advance into the age of technological efficiency, the wider the disparity grows."[4] Whereas most sectors are driven by the mass production of standardized goods and services, arts and culture offer singular performances and rare experiences, stimulating demand for limited editions and inimitable things rather than the same old commodities. The cost of creativity rises as the cost of automation lowers. That artistic products and cultural happenings are more expensive to make, and more pleasurable to consume, increases their value and worth.

As Toffler points out, each step toward "higher productivity in the economy at large pushes the arts back a step in terms of their peculiar handicraft economics."[5] Market forces did not magically invent this disparity once upon a time. The hands of government bureaucrats are all over it. That's the important point for City Hall: just as tax loopholes and giveaways entice business to produce more efficiently, so other policies can limit the encroachment of efficient production into arts and culture. On some level, DCA must simply accept responsibility for ensuring artistic and cultural livelihoods remain viable.

With Toffler probably on his mind, contemporary Brooklyn artist Joe Scanlan has riffed on long-term, inefficient careers in which artistic and cultural producers "shape the kind of market they want to inhabit" and expand "the value system of art and, by extension, the aesthetic of what "making money" looks like—the kinds of actions it might embody and the forms it might take."[6] He describes how "the real growth opportunities are in obscure enterprises where competition is low and materials cheap," and claims that "if art and independent contracting share anything it is the desire to minimize overhead costs."[7]

Toffler thought it was easiest to preserve inefficient careers through credits and incentives for thrill-seeking patrons rather than through subsidies requiring judgment to be exercised and taste to be legislated in ways that could thwart cutting-edge projects. "To expect federal subsidies to underwrite innovation or "way out" artistic enterprises is naïve," he reasoned, perhaps too stridently. "The same is true of city, county or state subsidies.... if we wish to encourage the spirit of experiment and risk-taking, the attitude of playfulness that is essential to art, we must enlarge the base of individual, as against collective, patronage."[8]

For all his insight, Toffler overlooked how government can champion daring activity and not get mired in debates over excellence and quality by facilitating situations and environments—scenes and milieus—in which new markets and enterprises can be lucratively developed and explored. That's what Elizabeth Currid reveals in her recent book, *The Warhol Economy: How Fashion, Art, and Music Drive New York City*.[9] She wins the prize for most fun had while doing research. Currid spent lots of time just hanging out with creative people, both famous and relatively unknown. She discovered that "formal institutions have not been particularly instrumental in artistic and cultural careers, even for those who have attained wide acclaim and credibility..."[10] No one she encountered had ever filled out a grant application or spoken with a DCA rep.

Instead, all these folks she got to know relied upon informal settings— always some nighttime joint, never a job fair or business workshop— to gain access to tastemakers and gatekeepers who helped them get ahead and plan their next move or learn where to find opportunities. The exchanges were unpredictable and freewheeling, like any good party. But they point to a pattern: social dynamics determine the economic behavior of people seeking artistic and cultural advancement.

In the fall of 2009, DCA announced major initiatives like expanding exhibition space in city-owned properties and increasing access to affordable performance space.[11] Worthwhile as these plans sound— and they are necessary—they won't get off the ground, the press release suggests, until other organizations manage the logistics and conduct outreach to artists and other designated beneficiaries.

Too often operations the agency could guide and control are effectively outsourced under the guise of empowering people to make decisions for themselves when, in fact, many artists and cultural producers are not affiliated with any particular institution or organization. Those among them who want more exhibition and performance space will still have to find it on their own. Now we come full circle: DCA staff must go out and reach people in the ephemeral settings and offbeat places where the creative economy thrives.

How about a grassroots operation in neighborhoods across the city, a fact-finding mission to grasp the latest artistic and cultural developments? Seriously: imagine enlisting eclectic purveyors of art and culture as native informants who could connect the agency directly to the concerns and interests of emerging and established creative leaders. Dialogue informed by first-hand knowledge of what's really happening in the field would open new avenues for government to respond to overlooked or misunderstood needs. Arts and culture policy would finally start to encompass more than the top-down administration of grants.

The example of indie rock promoter Todd Patrick is instructive. Anyone can get into the shows he organizes in Brooklyn and Queens in unglamorous, sometimes not fully legal, spots. The atmosphere is engaging and inviting: interactions and conversations tend to run late into the evening and almost naturally transcend the barriers of performance and spectatorship. Musicians and audience members at one show may well end up in a side outfit or new band by the next one.

Some of the biggest Brooklyn bands of the moment—Vivian Girls and Matt & Kim come to mind—cut their teeth playing these shows and remain connected to younger upstarts hoping to break through. Enough buzz and hype surround Patrick's gatherings that promoters operating in larger clubs and bars are obliged to follow his bookings religiously. As he gets closer to opening his own official venue, he is watching what the younger, less experienced kids are doing, those who learned from him but are putting their own stamp on things. A few months ago Patrick told NPR: "The scene is better for it. It's better now that tastemaker status and all that stuff has been kind of diluted and spread around. At the same time, I don't feel like my star has diminished. I feel like, you know, I still do great things, other people do great things. There's just great stuff happening."[12]

Patrick and company do it all themselves: finding spaces, negotiating with landlords, and getting the word out. Materials are cheap, competition low, and overhead minimal. Still, it's hard to sustain a living like this. Resourcefulness only carries you so far. A new motto, then, for DCA: here to lessen the difficulty.

Dan Morris *is director of communications at the Drum Major Institute for Public Policy.*

Endnotes

1   This is referenced in "Creative New York," a 2005 report by the Center for an Urban Future, p. 13: http://www.nycfuture.org/images_pdfs/pdfs/creative_new_york.pdf. And DCA's expense budget and capital budget are readily available online: http://www.nyc.gov/html/dcla/html/home/home.shtml.

2   "Arts as an Industry: Their Economic Impact on New York City and New York State," a 2007 report by Alliance for the Arts, p. 32: http://www.allianceforarts.org/pdfs/ArtsIndustry_2007.pdf.

3   Alvin Toffler, *The Culture Consumers: Art and Affluence in America* (Baltimore: Penguin Books, 1965).

4   *The Culture Consumers*, pp. 183–184, 215.

5   *The Culture Consumers*, p. 215.

6   Joe Scanlan, "Modest Proposals," *Artforum*, April 2008.

7 Joe Scanlan, "People in Trade, or, Forget Warhol," Things that Fall online forum: www.thingsthatfall.com.

8 *The Culture Consumers*, pp. 225–226.

9 Elizabeth Currid, *The Warhol Economy: How Fashion, Art, and Music Drive New York City* (Princeton: Princeton University Press, 2007).

10 *The Warhol Economy*, p. 112.

11 "Mayor Bloomberg Announces Five Initiatives to Help Strengthen New York City's Cultural Sector," September 30, 2009: http://www.nycedc.com/PressRoom/PressReleases/Pages/MayorBloombergAnnounces5InitiativestoStrengtenNYCulturalSector.aspx.

12 Josh Gleason, "Promoter Todd P is Getting His Own Place," National Public Radio, August 20, 2009: http://www.npr.org/templates/story/story.php?storyId=112066997.

WANTED: A COMMUNITY REINVESTMENT POLICY IN NEW YORK CITY
By Mark Winston Griffith

Policy makers and the financial services industry must make community reinvestment a cornerstone of any effort to rebuild the economies of New York's working class communities. I'm using "community reinvestment" to refer to any policy that determines that government- supervised or subsidized institutions have an obligation to return economic benefits to the public.

The Community Reinvestment Act (CRA) of 1977, which encourages federally regulated banks to meet the credit needs of all the communities they serve, including low- and moderate-income areas, is the definitive community reinvestment statute. New York City would be wise not only to resuscitate the letter and spirit of the CRA, which is an increasingly neglected and ineffective law, but consider applying it to a broader range of local industries, institutions, and practices.

In its heyday, during the 1980s and 1990s, the CRA was the driving force behind mostly positive relationships between local organizations and community stakeholders. Banks maintained active CRA offices that provided them with the institutionalized capacity to respond to pressing needs. These offices facilitated grants to community-based organizations, brokered multi-million dollar housing development partnerships, supported local merchant associations, and promoted aggressive mortgage and small business lending programs, just to name a few things.

CRA officers were like beat cops for the banks, keeping a finger on the pulse of the community, responding to civic calls for assistance, and helping to maintain the peace between banks and their customer base. Bank CRA offices were the clearing house for millions of dollars flowing into affordable housing, small business development, loan funds, credit unions, etc. In return, residents, community-based organizations and businesses gave these banks their business.

Community organizations and local leaders were empowered by the fact that they could challenge mergers and transactions that required regulatory approval. Activists like me tracked the business activities of banks and attended countless regulatory hearings in which we felt deputized to keep institutions accountable for their lending practices, or lack thereof. Although federal regulators in my experience never actually held up a merger because of a bank's CRA lapses, banks at least reacted as if they were being put on notice.

In case I'm waxing too nostalgic, let me admit that CRA offices in many instances served as glorified public relation arms of the banks. Also, the critique that community groups used the CRA to extort dollars from banks was not always unfounded. This was sometimes inevitable and simply the price of doing business, because CRA was in fact the only leverage point for community groups to get the attention of multi-billion dollar banking institutions.

Still, when functioning at its most effective level, CRA enabled banks to make strategic investment decisions based on collaborations with local organizations responsible for stimulating economic activity. Those decisions, when made well, helped provide housing, create and protect jobs, and inject badly needed credit and capital into communities and neighborhoods. The National Community Reinvestment Coalition estimates that trillions of dollars have been leveraged since 1977 in low- and moderate-income communities as a result of the CRA.

For years, the acknowledgment of community reinvestment responsibilities on the part of banks, even when superficial, shaped the conversation around community development, and connected words to deeds. But just as the opening and closing of bank branches, and terms like "redlining," and "Home Mortgage Disclosure Act" (HMDA) were on advocates' lips in the 1980s and 1990s, subprime loans, shady brokers, foreclosure rescue scams, and loan remediation dominated our attention in the 2000s. Today community reinvestment is no longer a stated goal for banks and regulators alike, so much so that few banks maintain active CRA offices anymore. With banks looking more to their multi-national profits, partnerships with local organizations have become low priority, and ad hoc.

It's easy to see how this dynamic has gone hand-in-hand with active disinvestment. Millions of dollars that could keep community-based organizations alive, employ people, and stimulate economic activity are now directed elsewhere. Furthermore, the hawking of high-priced loan products quickly became the default method of being responsive and "sensitive" to "high-risk" community needs. Working class neighborhoods of color like Central Brooklyn and Southeast Queens that should have been leading the way in an economic revival instead became drilling fields for exploitative gimmicks like "overdraft protection", refund anticipation loans, and exotic home equity products. If open and effective channels to bank regulators and banks had been kept intact, the abusive lending and real estate practices that we community reinvestment watchdogs complained about for years could have been addressed. Instead, because these complaints threatened the new business model and initial windfall profits of the banks, they were ignored or denied.

Any informed observer can recognize that, in recent years, the financial services infrastructure in NYC and throughout the country has stripped wealth and equity from the most vulnerable communities, rather than reinvest in them. Just consider the foreclosure crisis and the omnipresence of check cashing operations, rent-to-own stores, and payday lenders—particularly in urban neighborhoods of color—for painful verification of this assertion. It's no coincidence that savings rates and home equity levels among Americans are at record lows these days.

If you're looking for physical justification for community reinvestment, as well as a poetically tragic symbol of the trajectory that community-based finance has followed in New York, then travel with me to the northeast corner of Fulton Street and Bedford Avenue in Bed-Stuy Brooklyn.

Throughout the 1980s and early 1990s two conjoined brick buildings on this corner were home to a federally insured commercial bank. For decades it marginally served the surrounding community by taking deposits from its mostly low-and moderate Central Brooklyn customers without returning much in the way of credit. In 1993, that bank merged with another, closed several branches throughout New York City, and, through the prodding of the CRA, passed these two buildings onto the fledgling Central Brooklyn Federal Credit Union I had co-founded.

Using this large commercial space as a base of retail operations, the credit union was able to grow at a remarkable pace and convert deposits—made by local residents and from other banks similarly prodded by the CRA—into millions of dollars worth of loans and services that were used, among other things, to build businesses, send people to college and buy homes.

Unfortunately, the credit union couldn't afford the taxes and rent that came with the new real estate. So it had to move to another, smaller building in 1998. Today, one of these buildings is home to a lending institution that does not have any CRA obligations and does brisk business by charging local people usury rates to lease household furniture and appliances—the very antithesis of community reinvestment. Meanwhile, the bank that started off on that corner doesn't have a functioning community reinvestment program anymore, and the surrounding commercial and residential area, which has been the focus of countless revitalization efforts, is struggling.

We shouldn't let community reinvestment become a thing of the past. Fortunately, the National Community Reinvestment Coalition and other organizations have been working on CRA improvements for years. In devastated New York City neighborhoods, crucial areas of CRA advocacy must include: new criteria and standards that place a higher premium on relationships with local organizations; investments in civic and commercial revitalization; incentivizing job and affordable housing creation; more affordable pricing of products and services; and a proven commitment to consumer protection. Higher disclosure and transparency requirements that make it easier for local groups to access community reinvestment records and measure community reinvestment progress are also essential. Federal attempts to reform banking regulatory institutions must fully appreciate how much regulators have become deeply compromised by their dependence on the very institutions they are supposed regulate.

But the actual mechanics of a new commitment to community reinvestment in New York City are less important than summoning the political will to make community reinvestment a priority. That opportunity is upon us, in spite of the recent attempts by conservatives to discredit the CRA. In the wake of massive government bailouts of Wall Street and all the data and evidence available on abusive lending practices, public sentiment has never been more aligned with the concept of bank accountability and the notion that tax payers deserve a return on their investment. A more robust and enforceable CRA regime would have the power to proactively stimulate the economy, while flagging and guarding against destructive practices that threaten to strip further wealth and equity from struggling local communities and neighborhoods. The overarching goal of community reinvestment should be enabling local organizations to challenge and recover from the harmful actions of the banks that were responsible for leading us into this financial crisis.

Community reinvestment in New York should not begin and end with banks, though. Developers who receive public subsidies, for instance, are perfect candidates for a more comprehensive approach. Small community development projects, as well as high-profile, high-impact projects like Atlantic Yards, Willets Point, and the Mets and Yankee Stadium deals can, in the future, be converted into opportunities to aggressively redirect corporate profits toward community-based projects that have indisputable public benefits and spur new economic activity, thus pre-empting public opposition. Devices such as "clawbacks," community-benefit agreements, and inclusionary zoning already provide the precedent for development-related community reinvestment provisions. But they need to be strengthened and expanded.

Another element to consider is empowering a citywide office like the Public Advocate with the authority to monitor community reinvestment activity and compliance among banks, financial institutions, and developers. Although many believe New York City has little jurisdiction over corporate entities and federally regulated institutions, a determined and creative City Council, Public Advocate, or Mayor could challenge this assumption and find ways to apply local standards and increase accountability.

Community reinvestment is inseparable from economic recovery. If we don't find a way to recycle the profits, and police the activity, of financial institutions, developers, and other corporate institutions, corners like Fulton and Bedford will remain monuments to economic injustice and wasted potential.

Mark Winston Griffith is a former senior fellow in economic justice and executive director at the Drum Major Institute for Public Policy. He has been a community organizer and activist in Central Brooklyn for more than twenty years. During the fall 2009 election cycle, he ran for New York City Council to represent Central Brooklyn's 36th Council District.

CONCLUSION

By Dan Morris

Difficult work is underway. Everyone agrees that third-term poli-cymaking amid continued economic anxiety and uncertainty will not be easy. Meeting the challenges ahead requires a bold vision not just in the short run but for the long haul. The tasks and dilemmas exceed the confines of the annual budget cycle. For years to come, the ability of government to ensure a stable future for millions of New Yorkers will be tested.

It is time, then, for deliberation. Ideally, when we deliberate, we convey a willingness to change our minds. We examine assumptions, learn from each other, and figure out what to do by reconsidering and reevaluating what we thought we knew. This intellectual process, driven as it is by humility and honesty, can yield durable results, perhaps even robust coalitions where we discover areas of untapped potential and sources of strength that previously escaped us. That, at least, is our sincere hope here: to facilitate the best process and results of deliberation over how economic policy can enhance all lives, neighborhoods, and communities across our great city.

The diversity of the contributors reflects the organization that undertook this project. We are named after Dr. Martin Luther King Jr.'s sermon on the drum major instinct. Throughout his life, King harnessed the drum major instinct—which he defined as the desire "to be important, to surpass others, to achieve distinction, to lead the parade"—not for self-aggrandizement or material gain, but for selfless leadership. He stood out front to reframe polarizing debates and reshape entrenched views, enabling people to hear the rhythm of justice, fairness, and equality. New alliances guided by unifying ideas replaced old alliances shackled by prejudices of the past.

A movement was sustained.

Years ago, while recognizing that economic growth, development, and diversification affected his broad constituency, King emphasized that only government has the capacity to achieve the ideal of full employment, guaranteed annual income for all people. It must try to bring that aspiration closer to reality, he reasoned, because "if a man doesn't have a job or an income, he has neither life nor liberty nor the possibility for the pursuit of happiness. He merely exists." A sobering observation for us to consider today, especially at a time when thousands of people across the city are barely surviving.

When enough political will compels it, government can wield the power of policy to transform economic vulnerability into economic security. It can ensure people have good jobs that "pay them some money so they can live and educate their children and buy a home and have the basic necessities of life." It can raise the expectations of those at the bottom by creating "new forms of work that enhance the social good" and lift up people "for whom traditional jobs are not available." King believed in all this very deeply. We should recall how and why these convictions stirred him to act as he did.

He may not have put it like this, but he arguably saw government strengthening and expanding the middle class: it's where most people, whether they start on the lowest rungs of the ladder or a little higher, want to be. In our city, though, downward mobility is on the rise. Many who recently felt secure now struggle to get by; others somehow subsist on even less yet continue to imagine a better life.

This book is for all of them.

Dan Morris *is director of communications at the Drum Major Institute for Public Policy.*

About the Editors

Jonathan P. Hicks is a senior fellow at the DuBois Bunche Center for Public Policy (DBC) at Medgar Evers College, and a former political and financial reporter for *The New York Times*, where he covered the politics of New York and the role of people of color in the world of business for many years. During that time, he developed a reputation as one of the foremost authorities on the inner workings of the political culture in New York City and New York State. He has been a frequent guest on local radio and television news programs where he regularly offers political analysis and commentary. He recently received a Ford Foundation grant to travel to Liberia to write opinion articles and do reporting on the redevelopment of that West African country in the aftermath of its lengthy civil war and to begin developing a new journalism training program there.

Dan Morris is director of communications at the Drum Major Institute for Public Policy (DMI). A media strategist with a deep research and editorial background, he specializes in issue-based campaigns that shape news and opinion across many areas of policy and move progressive messages through the press and blogosphere. In recent years, his diverse portfolio has included urban policy, economic policy, environmental policy, education, the arts, and more. He has successfully pitched many competitive outlets in New York and Washington, including *The New York Times*, *The Washington Post*, *The Financial Times*, and *Politico*. He has also placed op-eds in newspapers around the country and essays in major magazines like *The Nation* and *The American Prospect*.

About DMI

The Drum Major Institute for Public Policy (DMI) is a nonpartisan, nonprofit think tank founded during the civil rights movement to put the best arguments and most effective tools into the hands of those advocating on the frontlines for progressive economic and social change. From the middle-class squeeze to comprehensive immigration reform to the economic potential of America's cities, DMI's research, analysis, media, and communications efforts shape how major policy debates are waged and won by elected officials, advocates, grassroots leaders, and concerned citizens at the local, state, and federal level. Always focused on winning the long-term battle of ideas, DMI trains talented young people from underrepresented communities to become the next generation of leaders who can advance progressive public policy. The organization changes the often insular conversation about policymaking by empowering diverse voices to drive it in new directions.

Please visit www.drummajorinstitute.org for more information.